For George Feirstein

"An affirmation and strength comes from a bonding between men that's impossible to put into words," says Ed Honnold, the mild-mannered federal lawyer and founder of the Men's Council of Greater Washington, one of six such local groups salving men's deep inner pain through communal rituals of dancing, roaring, hugging, and weeping. . . . "American men face a desperate situation and don't even know it." He pauses thoughtfully and adds, "There's a lot of hurtin' cowboys out there."

—From an article on the men's movement in the *Washington Post*, by reporter Phil McCombs

"This does not help our mission."

—Arnold Schwarzenegger, *Terminator 2*

BRUCE FEIRSTEIN

REAL MEN DON'T BOND

HOW TO BE A REAL MAN IN AN AGE OF WHINERS

ILLUSTRATED BY LEE LORENZ

WARNER BOOKS

A Time Warner Company

*Additional thanks are due Robert Collector, Mel Parker, Lary Simpson,
and Lois Wallace.*

Portions of this essay previously appeared in different form in Spy *magazine
and* TV Guide.

An excerpt of this essay appeared in Playboy.

The "bonding" quote on page one appears courtesy of the Washington Post,
© *1991, the* Washington Post, *used with permission.*

Warner Books, Inc., 1271 Avenue of the Americas, New York, NY 10020

W A Time Warner Company

Printed in the United States of America

First Printing: October 1992

10 9 8 7 6 5 4 3 2 1

Library of Congress Cataloging in Publication Data

Feirstein, Bruce.
    Real men don't bond: how to be a real man in an age of whiners /
Bruce Feirstein; illustrated by Lee Lorenz.
        p.   cm.
    ISBN 0-446-39463-7
    1. Men—Humor.   2. Masculinity (Psychology)—Humor.   I. Title.
PN6231.M4F37   1992
813'.54—dc20   92-14080
                                                                        CIP

Cover design by Michael Doret
Book design by H. Roberts

REAL MEN DON'T BOND

HOW TO BE A REAL MAN IN AN AGE OF WHINERS

1
The Return of Flex Crush

The phone rang at two-thirty in the morning.

"You up?" The voice at the other end of the line sounded like too many cigarettes, too many Slim-Jims, and far too many nights dining alfresco in the microwave section of a 7-Eleven in Eau Claire, Wisconsin.

"Who's this?"

"Flex," the voice said. "Flex Crush."

I bolted up in bed. I blinked. And suddenly it all came rushing back, fast and furiously, like the white-hot tip of an Exocet honing in on the ventilation shaft of a Baghdad bunker.

Flex Crush.

It had been ten years since I'd heard that name.

Ten years of Republicans in the White House.

Ten years of Japanese in our pocketbooks.

Ten years of Oprah and Phil, and GM still unable to make decent transportation.

Flex Crush.

An entire decade had passed since the self-proclaimed "Last Real Man in America"—a guy who drove nuclear waste for a living, and flossed with a chain saw—ten years had gone by since Flex descended from the mount of his Peterbilt 359 and delivered what he considered to be the last—and final—words on modern masculinity and the proper nutritional components for the Real Man's training table.

"Real Men don't eat bean curd, or tofu, or anything with 'lite' in the title," Flex had commanded. "Real Men don't have 'meaningful discussions.' They don't worry about giving somebody 'enough space.' They don't 'get into the mellow sound'; they don't contribute to PBS. Real Men only use rotary dial phones. What does a Real Man play on the piano? Poker. What does a Real Man eat for fruits and vegetables? Orange soda. How many Real Men does it take to cross a river? Five thousand. Four thousand nine hundred ninety-nine to build the suspension bridge, and one to drive across in the tractor-trailer."

Yes, it all came flooding back, like eleven million gallons of Exxon light crude lapping up on the shoreline of Prince William Sound.

Real Men don't need waterbeds.

Real Men aren't afraid to fly DC-10's.

Real Men don't trust France.

Or, put another way:

Real Men don't eat quiche.

"Never attempt with words what you can accomplish with a flamethrower," Flex had said that night, saluting as he eased his rig into the dawn.

Truly, words to live by.

More or less.

"What do you want?" I asked, fully aware of Flex's other edict: Real Men don't chat. They don't have time for small talk. There are just too many oil-rig fires that need capping, and far too many Chevys to recall. No "So how are the wife and kids?" No "So can you believe that Steinbrenner?" And certainly no "So how do you feel about that censorship issue, vis-à-vis the National Endowment for the Arts?"

No way.

Somewhere, as every Real Man knows, there's always some third world joker with a North Korean breeder-reactor that needs to be sought out, and destroyed, before lunch.

I heard Flex sigh.

"I'm pissed," he said at last. "We have to talk."

Shit. I was stricken. It wasn't that I didn't appreciate the phone call...

But you have to understand that after the last time we talked—after all that quiche hysteria—I swore, I swore up and down on a stack of Warren Commission reports that I'd never write about Flex Crush again. There were entire zip codes furious at me for pointing out that Nancy was the Real Man while Ronnie was asleep at the wheel; there were whole area codes of so-called firearms enthusiasts who insisted on calling at four o'clock in the morning to find out what kind of gun a Real Man carries. (Then again, maybe I was the idiot for answering them in the first place. "And what kind of gun are *you* carrying," I'd inquire politely. "Three-fifty-seven magnum," they'd invariably grunt. "Well far be it for me to say you're not a Real Man," I'd respond, and then try going back to sleep as they ranted and bellowed, "I know where you live, you son of a bitch!! What kind of Real Man is named Bruce?!?")

Yes, I wanted no part of it.

Not again.

But... well... on second thought...

Flex was pissed.

And if I never learned anything else in life, Flex had taught me two important lessons.

One: Real Men never let their friends down.

And two: Never turn your back on a guy who drives nuclear waste for a living. (Forget about the Scotts Four Season Turf Program. Let somebody put down a fine mulch of depleted uranium pellets on your front lawn, and not only is your crabgrass gone, but so are the snails, grubs, and most of the higher life forms in your immediate neighborhood. Trust me—it's hell on resale values.)

"Where do you want to meet?"

"Same place," he said.

I looked at my watch. Damn. Friend or not, it was two-thirty in the morning. Didn't Flex realize the eighties were over? Hadn't he heard it wasn't like the good old days—those halcyon, innocent times when we'd think nothing of staying up all night to console a friend (especially if he were a she) and still have the energy to be sitting with Mike Milken at that X-shaped desk at Drexel at six the next morning, all raring and ready to pillage and plunder the American economy into bankruptcy by noon?

"Do we have to do it tonight? Couldn't we get together for lunch? Or maybe drop me a fax?"

But as soon as the words were out of my mouth, I knew I'd made a mistake.

"Real Men don't fax," Flex snorted. "Real Men don't use E-Mail. Real Men don't modem, or have lunch, or agree to reconvene the committee at a later date," he said. "Real Men never put off till tomorrow what they can confront tonight, in the dark." He paused. "Be there."

"Yes sir."

"And bring a lawyer."

"What for? Don't you trust me?"

"Of course I trust you. I just need a chock for the front wheels of the truck."

Two hours later, I was sitting in the "Professional Drivers Only" section of the Vince Lombardi Rest Area on the New Jersey Turnpike. Like everywhere else in America, the past ten years had not been kind to the joint: Where there were once acres of genuine Formica, and heaping plates of "this'll stop your heart" bacon, eggs, and pancakes, the place now looked like the Cleveland Botanical Gardens, with carpeting, fake colonial wall trimmings, and an all-you-can-eat salad trough. Instead of a waitress named Madge (with an attitude to match), her name was Tiffany. She wore six earrings. In her *right* ear.

"What the hell happened here?" I asked.

She took off her Walkman. "What?"

"What happened?" I repeated. "This place used to have some style. Some personality."

Tiffany shrugged. "Corporate policy," she said. "They want every place to be the same. I think they think it makes people happy."

I nodded. She was right. As Flex had once complained, it's the death knell of local culture in America: Everywhere you go, everything looks the same. The same Footlocker, the same Radio Shack, the same Brookstone, Sharper Image, Pottery Barn, the same Dunkin' Donuts, the same McDonald's Playland. It doesn't matter whether you're in Ghirardelli Square in San Francisco, the Galleria in Baltimore, Faneuil Hall in Boston, Sixteenth Street in Denver, or the South Street Seaport in New York. It's all the same: America as one giant shopping mall and food court. Why bother going anywhere when you can go everywhere without leaving your own home?

"What'll you have?" Tiffany asked.

I was about to order when a voice boomed.

"No wimp food, now," I heard someone say. I looked up: It was Flex. He looked older. And thinner. Was that a Gap T-shirt he was wearing?

"Bring us two cups a' Joe, honey," Flex said, smiling as he slid into the booth. "And a croissant. No— make that a fruit salad."

Croissants? Fruit salad? Flex Crush eating anything but a dead animal? No bacon? No fries? Was the last vestige of American Manhood hopelessly lost to politically correct foods? My faith in him was sinking faster than consumer confidence during the Bush administration.

"Gotta watch my cholesterol," Flex explained. "And I'm off the pig."

Suddenly I had that sinking feeling in the hollow of my stomach—that "how the hell did this happen?" sensation so well known to anybody with a middle-class income during the past four years.

"Off the pig?"

"Yeah," Flex sighed. "My new partner told me all about nitrocimines. And trichinosis. His name's Ahmad. He's a good guy. He's a Muslim."

Flex Crush, driving with a Muslim partner?

Flex Crush, watching his cholesterol?

"Hey, what can I say?" Flex shrugged. "I'm the last of a dying breed. White Eurocentric male."

Just then, Tiffany appeared with the coffee and fruit salad. I was almost afraid to ask the next question.

"Do you still drive nuclear waste for a living?"

Flex waved it aside with his fork. "Nah. I'm in the recycling business."

"The *recycling* business?"

"Yeah. Got me a load a' empties outside, gotta be in Memphis by sundown."

I was astounded.

"Don't look so surprised," Flex said, glancing up from his fruit salad. "Real Men adapt to the times. It's like the dinosaurs and the Democratic party: If you don't change, you die."

Over the next ten minutes, Flex told me the story of his life during the past decade: How he'd been stuck in traffic on the 605 freeway in Los Angeles for three years, trying to get off at the City of Industry exit ("The whole damned country's turning into a giant parking lot"); how he got into the recycling business ("Remember Ross Johnson, the CEO of RJR Nabisco, from the book *Barbarians at the Gate*? The guy who had *eleven* corporate jets? He bought my company in a hostile takeover in '86. I thought I was going to be hauling Oreos for a living. Remember the way he supposedly sent his dog around in an empty corporate jet? Forget it. I was following him everywhere with a grand piano. Eventually I quit—but not before my division was spun off to a South Korean shipping conglomerate.") And finally, the saga of how his marriage weathered the decade, after his kids moved out, and his wife took a job leasing commercial office space for Century 21 in downtown Houston. ("After the real estate market crashed in '87, she took a night course in 'Self-actualization and Important Female Writers of the 20th Century,'" Flex explained, "and she eventually opened a Mail Boxes Etc. franchise on Travis Street. We're still married," he said. "And sooner or later, I wouldn't be surprised if we ended up living together again.")

Ah, the eighties. I could sympathize with the man. In the end, it hadn't turned out to be an easy time for anybody, with the possible exception of investment bankers and savings-and-loan officers, most of whom were now coming up for parole.

Still, it was time to get down to business.

"So what's bothering you?" I asked.

Flex sat back in his seat. Pushed off his fruit salad. Cracked his knuckles. And frowned.

"Men."

"Men?"

"Men," he said again. "I thought we straightened all this stuff out ten years ago. But nobody seemed to listen."

"What do you mean?"

"Bonding."

"What?"

"Bonding," he repeated. "Jerks running round the forest, banging on drums, chanting to get in touch with their manhood."

I nodded.

"Pretty boys on Harleys."

I nodded again.

"Guys trying to find their masculinity at seminars."

I nodded a third time.

"Former congressmen lobbying for the Japanese. IBM's screw-ups. Bryant Gumbel's memos. Alan Dershowitz's clients. Mario Cuomo playing Hamlet, Calvin Klein's advertising, Oliver Stone's self-righteousness."

He paused.

"Guys in suits on rollerblades."

Flex shook his head in disgust.

"I'm pissed," he said for the third time that night, and then proceeded to clarify the statement:

"The problem today isn't wimps, or Phil Donahue, or even quiche.

"The problem is that we've become a nation of whiners.

"Special interest groups.

"Political action committees.

"Publicity hounds.

"Professional victims who blame their problems on everybody but themselves.

"Fat-cat military contractors who bitch and moan because peace has broken out.

"Titanic corporations like GM and Chrysler who whine and bellyache about Japanese imports—when the simple truth of the matter is that it's their own damn fault: They don't make cars we want to buy."

The entire restaurant had fallen silent. It was so quiet you could hear the radar detectors going off in the eighteen-wheelers on the turnpike.

"Look," Flex said, "We don't make TV's anymore—we make class action suits. We don't join communities—we form 'prisoners' rights' advocacy groups—and then argue about calling them 'convicted maniacs,' or 'the differently freedomed.'"

He shook his head.

"Let me tell you something," he continued, in a voice that indicated I didn't have much choice in the matter, "it all comes down to this:

"Real Men don't whine.

"Real Men don't bond.

"Real Men recognize you can't have rights without responsibilities.

"This whole men's movement is nonsense. Real Men aren't worried about finding their masculinity, they're worried about paying off their MasterCard bills.

"When a Real Man wants to bond he uses a Black and Decker glue gun.

"When a Real Man wants to get in touch with his 'primordial self,' he burns fossil fuel. On a highway. In a tractor-trailer. Carrying blue-carbon steel.

"And there's one other thing—"

"What's that?"

"*The only time Real Men chant is at third and short yardage.*"

Ah, yes. This was the Flex I knew and loved: the Last Real Man—the Last Real Angry Man in America.

Flex stood up. "Look," he said finally, "it's almost impossible to get anything done in this country today without offending somebody. I apologize to women, the snail darter, and *anybody* who's pissed off about Christopher Columbus. But we've got bridges to fix, AIDS to cure, homeless to house, and the average nine-year-old can't read a stop sign without a remedial reading course.

"Let's get on with it."

As Flex went out to check on the lawyer under the front wheels of his truck, I began to write down some questions.

Is it possible to be a Real Man in an age of soft targets, cellular phones, politically correct history, and collateral damage?

Is it really conceivable for mere mortals to uphold the standards of Clint, Sly, the Duke, and Arnold in an era of incorrect TRW credit reports, Islamic Jihads, and mindless drive-by killings?

Flex promised the answers to all this—and more—when he returned.

"Just remember one thing," he said before he left. "Real Men do not go into the woods to get naked, hug each other, and communicate around a campfire."

"Why not?"

"What the hell do you think the Winnebago and a Bud suitcase was invented for?"

I signaled Tiffany for another cup of coffee.

It was going to be a long night.

"In this family, son, bonding means
tax-free municipals."

2

Real Man Quiz #1

Q: How many Real Men does it take to change a light bulb in America today?

A: None. Because the minute a Real Man even gets near the bulb, you can bet your ass that somehow twenty-six lawyers from the ACLU are going to show up, suing to protect the interests of one jerk who claims he has a "Constitutional right" to be left sitting in the dark.*

---

*Actually, this is the abbreviated version of the joke. The full-length (or, as they'd say in Hollywood, the uncut director's version) goes like this:

Q: How many Real Men does it take to change a light bulb in America today?
A: Zero. But it takes 345 people to determine this, broken out as follows:
One guy to notice the bulb is out; six bureaucrats to refuse responsibility for it; one director of light bulb affairs to convene a "high-level commission" to investigate if the bulb really needs changing; sixteen people to sit on the committee; four lawyers and six community leaders to challenge the sexual, economic, and racial makeup of the committee; thirty-two politically correct persons to sit on the new committee; eleven consultants to write the initial report; six linguists to put it in Spanish, Italian, and Serbo-Croatian; four administrative assistants to photocopy the report, and one guy to fix the copier.
Then: nine new members of the committee to replace the nine members who resigned in disagreement over the first report; and one federal judge to rule that the light bulb must—in fact—be changed.
Next, twenty-six attorneys to file the environmental-impact statement; nine lighting consultants to write up the specifications for the new bulb; five engineers to write up the specifications for the ladder; one member of the Department of Commerce who flies to Japan using the "light bulb affair" as a wedge to reopen U.S./Japan trade agreements; eleven lawyers ("in-house counsel") to write the contract; twelve other lawyers ("out-house counsel") to rewrite the contract at $350 per hour; fourteen community leaders who sue to make sure the contract goes to someone with the correct sexual/economic/racial background; eight Human Resources Administrators who are hired to ensure compliance with the "above-stated regulation"; nine union guys who threaten to "shut the whole damn city down" if they're not allowed to bid on the contract; five investigative journalists to break the story; and Felix Rohatyn to settle the whole mess.
Then: sixty-two lawyers and thirty-seven insurance adjusters to settle the negligence claims from people who broke their legs falling due to the lack of light; fifteen people to serve on a new high-level commission to review "the way we do business," and six PR writers to create the press release announcing, "At long last, the light bulb will be changed."
And finally: twenty-six ACLU lawyers who successfully sue to protect the interests of one jerk who claims he has a constitutional right to be left sitting in the dark.
Happy? Good. Now go out and buy the colorized version.

3

The Real Man, Redefined

Ten years ago, it was easy to think you were a Real Man.

You raided corporations with junk bonds; you stripped 'em down, broke 'em up, spun 'em off, and dumped the first wife for a twenty-six-year-old blonde with an MBA.

You said you were "mentoring her."

You ate power breakfasts with powerful people; you penciled-in power lunches with power brokers.

You carried a platinum American Express card, but put the charges on Optima.

You identified closely with a novel about life under the bright lights of the big city that was narrated by, yes, "You."

You didn't marry, you merged. If you were single, you slept with everything in sight.

You wore power suits, power ties, power shoes, power socks, and did your inside trading at a bank in the Cayman Islands.

You thought you were a Real Man.

You were wrong.

"Real Men don't plea-bargain," said Flex. "Real Men

"Let's get this straight, Thatcher. Here at Marley, Low, and Warren, we have no intention of getting in touch with our inner child."

pour cement; they don't 'live off the fees.' The Real Man's parachute is made of silk, not gold. And as every Real Man knows, when it comes to a power lunch, there's only one meal that fits the bill: a bunch of guys eating subs, on a sub."

Yes, the "To Have, and Have More" decade is over.

The world is a different place today: Most of Europe—including the French—are actually on speaking terms. What's left of the USSR wants to join NATO. (Who knows? Maybe they like the dental plan.) And the Japanese have not only achieved domination in consumer electronics, but have taken the World Cup in sexism.

The nation cries out for leadership.

For vision.

For affordable cable television.

So what is it, then, that defines the Real Man today?

What separates him from the whiners, the people who produce "A Current Affair," and future Supreme Court nominees who hang around the water cooler discussing Long Dong Silver?

"Real Men don't have phone sex," said Flex.

"Real Men are not 'searching for the child within.'

"Real Men don't need spin control.

"Real Men always had a moral compass that points true north," said Flex. "They understand it's not how many corporations you gut, or how much ink you get. In the end, a man is judged by his deeds."

Donald Trump—by any criteria—is not a Real Man.

Jimmy Carter turned out to be a Real Man, while Jerry "What time do we tee off?" Ford did not.

John Sununu tried hard to be a Real Man. Too hard.

What else?

Real Men are, well, Real.

Real Men are not members of the Hair Club for Men.

They don't join the Players Club with Telly Savalas.

Real Men don't talk about their "life-style"; they don't get "chronic fatigue syndrome"; they don't believe in the "healing power of crystals."

For Real Men, the working definition of "dysfunctional" is New York City.

And "co-dependent" is two guys carrying an I beam.

Real Men don't brag about the number of women they've slept with, the number of people they've laid off, or the number of times they've played golf with Dan Quayle.

(Would you?)

Real Men are not "hooked on phonics"; they don't watch advertorials; they don't badger their friends, neighbors, and co-workers to become Nu Skin distributors.

(Robert Vaughn and Ali McGraw notwithstanding, Real Men don't trust anything marketed on television as "the system.")

Real Men have their houses insulated to R-38, and their TV sets tuned to CNN...

(Although even Real Men can't believe anybody would actually *buy* a Rolling-Writer to make graph paper.)

Real Men don't own the Abdomenizer, Thigh Cruncher, or eight-hundred-dollar mountain bikes. ("It's the supreme example of technology gone insane," he said. "Have you tried to buy a simple bicycle lately? It's worse than a VCR loaded with nonsense like six-year-in-advance two-thousand-event programming." Flex paused. "Actually, it isn't the cost of the bike that kills you. It's the SWAT team you have to hire to guard it.")

Real Men compost. They work on the line. They don't have a "fall color pallet." (For Real Men, the primary colors are battleship gray, camouflage, and anything that comes in a can marked Rust-oleum.)

Real Men don't spend twenty-eight dollars on designer T-shirts ("Real Men's T-shirts are built by somebody named Hanes," insisted Flex), and they don't buy two-hundred-dollar sneakers. ("The whole idea of 'cross-training shoes' is absurd," said Flex. "What is a forty-year-old in training *for*? The fifty-yard shopping-bag lug from the check-out counter? Wind-sprints to the cash machine?" He shook his head and focused on his other pet peeve: sports stars endorsing those same two-hundred-dollar sneakers. "Real Men know the answer to the question 'Is it the shoes, is it the shoes?'" said Flex. "Yes, it's the shoes you're pushing that kids are killing each other for in the ghetto.")

Real Men don't buy Calvin Klein jeans—and wish someone would tell dear Calvin that Real Men wear their jeans—they don't wipe their genitals with them.

And they think maybe it's time to rethink the National Endowment for the Arts. ("If you want to smear chocolate all over your body, be my guest," said Flex. "But let's not get confused here: You don't have a 'constitutional right' to make me pay for it.")

And even Real Men today find most beer commercials not only sexist, but insulting.

To men.

Real Men, you see, have a sense of propriety. And perspective. They realize there's more to life than revenge, and a cellular phone paid for by the company.

Real Men in the media (yes, it's hard to believe, but there are some) don't act as prosecutor, judge, and jury. They don't ask lurid questions about a candidate's sex life; they don't pay the alleged "other woman" to spill the beans.

(And before we get in too deep here, Real Men have no use for *any* presidential candidate who masquerades as a choir boy. But at the same time, they're none too thrilled by reporters who ask questions like "Did you have a threesome?" and "Did he use a condom?" under the guise of "the public's right to know." Real Men—and Real Reporters—understand the difference between the importance of dirty linen and, say, nuclear Armageddon. "And as far as the drug question goes," said Flex, "do we really want to elect somebody who wasn't even the least bit curious about marijuana in the sixties?")

Real Men aren't fooled by the phrase "surgical strike," or the current euphemism for "massive, unprecedented, economy-crippling firings" known as "downsizing."

They don't waste years of their lives playing make-believe baseball in rotisserie leagues.

They don't watch "American Gladiators."

They don't spend more for a car than their parents spent on the house they grew up in. And they don't drive Porsches.

Real Men—at forty—don't blame their current problems on the fact that their fathers didn't take them to a Dodgers game when they were twelve.

Real Men—at forty—aren't single.

Real Men don't care who killed Laura Palmer.

And Real Men don't *need* to schedule "quality time" with their children.

("Give me a break," said Flex. "If you have to schedule quality time with your kids, forget about the college tuition fund. Start saving—now—for the psychoanalysis.")

Real Men don't earn their livings off the misfortunes of the Kennedys or Marilyn Monroe. They were not amused by Clarence Thomas posing with the Bible in *People* magazine. They're not fascinated by the latest epic events in the press-release lives of Madonna, Cher, Don Johnson, or Michael Jackson.

(True, Michael might not categorize himself as a Real Man. But on the other hand, Real Men do wonder: If—as his song goes—"It doesn't matter if you're black or white," why does photographic evidence of him indicate otherwise?)

Real Men have become increasingly suspicious of the arch—and, let's say high-handed—attitude of certain members of the media; as long as we're in the mood to "kick the bums out," Real Men have begun to think that maybe it's time to consider term limits on pundits and network interviewers.

And finally, Real Men have absolutely no sympathy for John Gutfreund, Clark Clifford, Charles Keating, Dennis Levine, Ivan Boesky, or Mike Milken.

Especially Milken.

"He admitted he was guilty," said Flex. "End of story. Real Men don't plea-bargain, and then hire Alan Dershowitz to whine about it."

Flex pushed himself back from the table.

"You leave anything out?" I asked.

"Four things," he said.

"Real Men are not afraid of Islamic Jihads.

"Real Men are not writing a screenplay.

"Real Men *still* don't trust the French.

"And Real Men don't kid themselves: They don't spend twenty-eight bucks on tube socks at J. C. Penney, and think it's going to stimulate the economy."

He sat back.

He looked at the list.

"Jesus," he said. "It's almost enough to make you want to go out into the forest and bang on some drums."

WHAT REALLY PISSES REAL MEN OFF

(% of day they're pissed off about it)

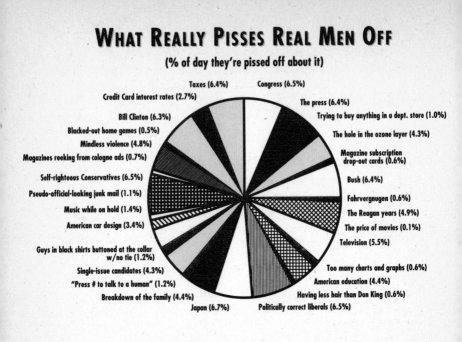

- Taxes (6.4%)
- Credit Card interest rates (2.7%)
- Bill Clinton (6.3%)
- Blacked-out home games (0.5%)
- Mindless violence (4.8%)
- Magazines reeking from cologne ads (0.7%)
- Self-righteous Conservatives (6.5%)
- Pseudo-official-looking junk mail (1.1%)
- Music while on hold (1.4%)
- American car design (3.4%)
- Guys in black shirts buttoned at the collar w/no tie (1.2%)
- Single-issue candidates (4.3%)
- "Press # to talk to a human" (1.2%)
- Breakdown of the family (4.4%)
- Japan (6.7%)
- Congress (6.5%)
- The press (6.4%)
- Trying to buy anything in a dept. store (1.0%)
- The hole in the ozone layer (4.3%)
- Magazine subscription drop-out cards (0.6%)
- Bush (6.4%)
- Fahrvergnugen (0.6%)
- The Reagan years (4.9%)
- The price of movies (0.1%)
- Television (5.5%)
- Too many charts and graphs (0.6%)
- American education (4.4%)
- Having less hair than Don King (0.6%)
- Politically correct liberals (6.5%)

WHO/WHAT THEY BLAME FOR THE BREAKDOWN OF AMERICAN SOCIETY

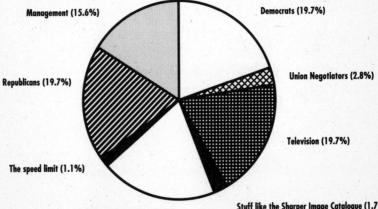

- Management (15.6%)
- Republicans (19.7%)
- The speed limit (1.1%)
- The Press (19.7%)
- Democrats (19.7%)
- Union Negotiators (2.8%)
- Television (19.7%)
- Stuff like the Sharper Image Catalogue (1.7%)

4
Real Man Quiz #2

Q: What's the Real Man's definition of a power tie?

A: 220-volt service.

Q: What's the Real Man's idea of a power suit?

A: Aces over kings.

"Miss Harper, this is a little something to mark our
fifty-five years together, and if I have ever been
guilty of sexual innuendos, I hope you will find it
in your heart to forgive me."

5

Four Things You'll Never Find in a Real Man's House

1. Nintendo
2. Super Nintendo
3. A Filofax
4. Martha Stewart's guide to home entertaining.*

---

*In truth, the full list also includes balloon curtains, a Yorkshire terrier, hair gel, Windham Hill CDs, postage stamps, whale recordings, a Dustbuster, something called "I-can't-believe-it's-not-butter," and anything that might be referred to as a "nice, fruity '89 Chardonnay." The explanation for the brevity of the main list is because anything longer might require one of those cute pastel-colored "Things to Remember" pads—which is yet something else you won't find in a Real Man's house.

6

The Flex Crush Industrial Index of Real Men

So just who are today's Real Men?

Who meets the criteria of Mossad, the Royal Canadian Mounted Police, Tom Clancy, *and* Flex Crush?

Who embodies the integrity of Lassie, the strength of Shamu, the intelligence of Flipper, the resilience of—

"Hey—go easy with that animal stuff," groused Flex. "Wait a minute. I *groused*? Didn't I just tell you—"

Okay, okay.

Basically, the World According to Flex is divided into two categories: Real Men, and Whiners. The main distinction being that a Real Man is the guy you'd be lucky to get stuck on a lifeboat with, while the Whiner is your worst nightmare—your Donald Trump, if you will—of the same event.

Colin Powell, for example, is a Real Man.

Lee "Banzai!" Iacocca has turned into a Whiner.

Sean Connery—a Lion in Winter—is a Real Man; Orrin Hatch, Arlen Specter, and Howard Metzenbaum may be called many things, but Real Man isn't one of them.

"You have reached Senator Carlton's office. If you're calling to condemn his environmental policy, press one. If you're calling to renounce his vote on defense, press two. And if you'd like to launch a personal attack on his character, press star."

Nolan Ryan, still pitching in his forties, and not complaining about the money or the pain is a Real Man.

Harrison Ford, Danny Glover, Mel Gibson, Bill Hurt, Gregory Hines and Tom Berenger all fit the bill. (They do the job, even if it means getting blown up on a toilet seat.)

Somebody like Sean Penn is a whiner. ("Grow up. You can't have it both ways," said Flex. "You *chose* to become an actor—a career that virtually screams 'look at me.' You *chose* to marry Madonna. Paparazzi come with the territory. Deal with it.")

All of the Bridges are Real Men: Lloyd, Beau, Jeff, Seattle-Tacoma.

Ditto anyone named Douglas.

Also Quaid, Marsalis, and the Wayans family.

Lowell Weicker, governor of Connecticut, is a Real Man; Mario Cuomo is too indecisive—and too hyper-sensitive—to qualify. (Real Men, and Real Democrats, don't wait for a hand-delivered invitation from God to run for president. And they don't come up with some candy-assed excuse about *not* running because the junior Republican state legislator from the Ninth Congressional District outside of Scarsdale wouldn't let them balance the state budget. Let's face it: This wouldn't have stopped Ike, Truman, Bobby Kennedy, or even Jerry Brown.)

Charles Kuralt, David Brinkley, Eric Sevareid, and John Chancellor are Real Men; the correspondents on "60 Minutes" are Real Men most of the time—and 100 percent of the time compared to the correspondents on "Hard Copy."

Mike Ditka is—obviously—a Real Man.

Ted Turner is a Real Man, even though he's wrong about colorizing old films. (Real Men *like* things in black & white.)

And George Steinbrenner is the scourge of major league baseball, professional athletics, the United

States, the western hemisphere, the earth, the solar system, and all of the presently charted galaxies.

He's also a whiner.

("Don't hold back on me here," I said to Flex. "I want to know what you really think."

"What I really think," he replied, "is there are too many people today who fit into the 'how do you sleep?' category; too many people who deserve to run into someone like Joseph Welch, the attorney who brought Joe McCarthy down by asking, 'Have you no sense of decency, sir, at long last? Have you no sense of decency?'")

Real Men are the guys we look up to; they don't sell out, they weren't on the board of the Bank of Credit and Commerce International; they do more with their lives than capriciously trade baseball players, and figure out ways to sell SAMs and cluster bombs to third world nations.

Joe Pesci, John Candy, and Harvey Keitel are all Real Men. Ditto Alec Baldwin, Rick Moranis and Bruno Kirby. And you get the same feeling about Patrick Swayze: He seems to be a guy who always tries to do his best.

Paul Harvey, the radio commentator, might as well have a business card that reads, "Paul Harvey, Real Man."

On the basis of the choices they've made in their work, Dustin Hoffman, Robert Redford, and Paul Newman are all Real Men—as are Richard Dreyfuss, Martin Landau, Steve Martin, Tom Hanks, and Jason Robards. But Real Men have begun to worry about Jack Nicholson. ("*Children?* Commitment?" Flex was incredulous. "How the hell is he going to get to Lakers games?")

Among the network anchors, there's no question about Bernard Shaw, Tom Brokaw, and Peter Jennings —although Dan Rather seems to fluctuate. (Real Men are especially fond of Brokaw's wardrobe: It's the most reliable indicator of world events. If he's in the turtleneck and the Patagonia windbreaker, you know it's either a coup or a war; but if he's rigged out in pinstripes, it's probably nothing more important than an economic summit, and you can go back to watching "America's Most Wanted" secure in the knowledge that the American Way of Life will probably make it through the half hour.)

CNN's Charles Jaco is a Real Man; Wolf Blitzer gets the nod on his name alone. But much as we'd like to include Arthur Kent, he has to lose the nickname: Real Men are not called the "Scud Stud"—although they are called "Forrest Sawyer."

And between Annette Bening and Warren Beatty, the choice should be obvious.

Roseanne Arnold tries hard to be a Real Man, but John Goodman is truly the Real Thing.

Jimmy Connors has become a grown-up Real Man.

But Bryant Gumbel just doesn't get it. ("Real Men have grown just a wee bit tired of the semiannual hysteria over his contract negotiations," Flex sighed. "Real Men don't assassinate via interoffice memo. In the grand scheme of things, Willard Scott—who is a Real Man—doesn't take *himself* that seriously.")

Ralph Lauren dresses up like a Real Man—but Real Men suspect otherwise, and believe that one day (using his advertising as evidence) the Israeli Knesset will convene a tribunal to try him for "massive crimes committed against the Jewish people by promoting Aryan stereotypes."

And no one, of course, is going to call Don King *anything*.

What else?

Real Men did not vote for David Duke in Louisiana. (Real Louisianians understand the difference between a Real Man and a Real Nightmare.)

Or Michael Dukakis in '88. ("Give me a break," said Flex. "The man's wife admits she's been drinking everything but nail polish remover for twenty-three years and he didn't have an inkling about it? Was this the guy we wanted in charge of the Strategic Air Command?")

Real Men have no use for self-aggrandizing celebrities. ("Hey," said Flex. "If you really wanted to do something to promote the peace after the L.A. riots, instead of making photo-op public service television commercials, why don't you *stop* making movies and TV shows filled with racist stereotypes and gratuitous violence?")

Real Men have no sympathy for anybody who fits into the "compulsive confessors" category—those stars who announce they've kicked drugs, overcome bulimia, or suddenly remember their abusive parents during network ratings periods, or the week they have a movie opening. (Flex: "The only thing these people are really addicted to is public attention, which brings up the great existential question of the nineties: If a celebrity makes some kind of shocking confession— and nobody hears about it—does that make them less of a celebrity?")

And there are no Real Men in the National Rifle Association. ("Hey," said Flex, "I like to hunt and fish as much as anybody. But everyone knows there's only one use for an AK-47—and the problem is that too many damned disgruntled post office workers have found out exactly what that is."*)

Real Men aren't smug; they're not thugs, braggarts, or showboats.

Barbara Bush is a Real Man—and Real Men suspect

---

*This led to one of Flex's more colorful digressions of the evening: "Just imagine," he said. "Malibu declares itself a 'nuclear-free zone'—which, of course, makes *everyone* think twice before setting off an atomic bomb on the Pacific Coast Highway. But the NRA, ever vigilant in their crusade to protect the average high school drop-out's right to pack enough firepower to waste a North Korean armored battalion—or a K mart—sues, claiming the 'right to bear arms' can't be abridged, including the right to 'bear nuclear arms.' And no doubt they'll find a rabbit rancher in El Monte who *swears* he uses a 10K thermonuclear device to cull his herd." Flex sighed. "These days, their initials stand for 'No Responsibility Accepted.' But on the other hand, who knows? The way things are going, maybe the post office should just try to improve morale by issuing a special 'Mass Murderers of the Postal Service' commemorative series."

that the country might indeed be a kinder, gentler nation if her husband listened to her more often.

Bob Hoskins is a Real Man, irrespective of his costar, Roger Rabbit, who is unquestionably a whiner. (Honestly: Is Roger really in the same league as Bugs, Yosemite Sam, or even Wilma Flintstone? When Bugs gets slammed by an anvil, or crushed by a bank safe, he picks himself up and goes on. Roger Rabbit's the kind of guy who files for workman's comp.)

Craig T. Nelson from "Coach" is a Real Man; as is Gerald McRaney from "Major Dad"—although Real Men would prefer to be known as "sir," or, in a pinch, "Supreme Allied Commander."

Sharpe James, the Mayor of Newark, is a Real Man, with a Real Man's name, in a Real Man's job.

And no list of Real Men would be complete without Nick Nolte, Richard Widmark, Robert Stack, Johnny Carson, Carl Weathers, Charles Durning, Louis Gossett, Billy Wilder, Ossie Davis, Michael Caine, Burt Lancaster, Gregory Peck, Sidney Poitier, Gene Hackman, Harry Dean Stanton, the editors of *Popular Mechanics*, Kathleen Turner, and Norman Schwarzkopf, as a general.

Then there's Geraldo.

How do we wince at Geraldo?

Let us count the ways: His TV shows, his book, his—

"Oh, forget it," Flex said, dismissing the subject with a wave of his hand. "It's just not worth the paper."

Flex was silent.

"Let me throw two names at you," I said.

"I wouldn't have it any other way."

"Bart Simpson?"

"Get serious. I got a truck a' empties outside waiting to get melted."

"Okay. Sly Stallone?"

Flex flexed. "Real Man."

"Really?"

"Sure. He's been up, he's been down, he's been humble, he's been arrogant, he's made an ass of himself, he's screwed up his marriages."

"So?"

"If you were twenty-eight and had won the Oscars for *Rocky*, could you have handled your life any better?"

"No, but—"

"No 'buts.' I guarantee that *in our lifetime*, we'll see Sly as revered as John Wayne or Clint, film retrospectives and all. The point is that he keeps trying. Can you come up with a better definition of a Real Man?"

I had to admit, Flex had a point.

(About three hundred of them, by my count.)

If you require further clarification, this may help:

Real Men

Arnold	Raul Julia	Denzel Washington
Joe Don Baker	Joe Mantegna	Robert Mitchum
Stephen Hawking	Barbara Bush	Don Ameche
James Earl Jones	Wesley Snipes	Dennis Farina
Regis and Kathie Lee	Jack Palance	Larry Fishburne
Brian Dennehy	Václav Havel	Fred Ward
Rubén Blades	Damon Wayans	Tom Seaver
Bob Woodward	Edward James Olmos	Bonnie Raitt
Armand Assante	Larry Kramer	Morgan Freeman
Molly Ivins	Ned Beatty	Robert Prosky
Harry Belafonte	Claude Akins	John Singleton
Scott Glenn	Ray Charles	

Guys Who Think They're Real Men, but Definitely Aren't

Norman Mailer	Oliver Stone	Axl Rose
Andrew Dice Clay	Daryl Gates	Marilyn Quayle

Guys Who Try Hard, but Just Can't Seem to Get the Hang of It

Sam Skinner, Sam Donaldson, Bob Mosbacher, and Ron Brown

Guys Who Try Too Hard

Steven Seagal

Guys Who Just Don't Have a Clue

Mickey Rourke, the Senate Judiciary Committee

Guys Who Are Probably Real Men, but We're Still Not Sure Of

Dick Cheney, Camille Paglia

Whiners, Ink Junkies, and Other Things Real Men Find Too Embarrassing to Talk About in Polite Company

Donald Trump	Gary Hart	Alan Dershowitz
Marion Barry	LaToya Jackson	Hands Across America
Jeff Koons	Kitty Kelly	William Kunstler
Julia Phillips	Michael Jackson	Jessica Hahn
1984–1989	Leona Helmsley	Gennifer Flowers

Connie Chung and Maury Povich
And
NFL Football in August
Wilt Chamberlain's Sex Life
Tommy Lasorda's weight problems
The entire House of Representatives
Simi Valley
Chris "If it's flat, I'll sell ads on it" Whittle
John "There is no hole in the ozone" Sununu
Arizona's refusal to celebrate Martin Luther King's birthday

Four Things You're Guaranteed to Find in Every Real Man's House

1. Caulk
2. Snow tires
3. A coffee can filled with loose screws
4. The Victoria's Secret Catalog*

*For the sake of brevity—and because Real Men know that any household list longer than this usually includes 'taking out the garbage,' we've limited it to four. But you'll also find a fire extinguisher, a miter box, finishing nails, jumper cables (in the house, never the car), a Shop-vac, a chin-up bar, the J.C. Whitney catalog, Jack Daniels, a rental receipt for the long version of *The Godfather*, microwave popcorn, paint chips, a VCR blinking 12:00, one bottle of champagne, a clock radio blinking 12:00, and the three things every Real Man wishes he could name his sons after, as in "Meet my boys: Armor-All, WD-40, and Rust-oleum."

"...and if you're feeling guilty about the oppressive, stifling, and culturally bankrupt history of colonialist, Eurocentric civilization, our politically correct special of the day is the non-western omelet."

8

Real Men and Politics

*I*n 1835, after a year-long tour of America, the French writer Alexis de Tocqueville predicted that democracy would only attract second-raters to serve in the government.

(And lest there be any confusion, let's establish two facts up front: 1) the Iowa caucuses, the AFL-CIO, Larry King, and the Arsenio Hall Show were not yet a factor in presidential politics, and 2) Tocqueville presumably wasn't here looking for the Jerry Lewis or Mickey Rourke of the age.)

Nevertheless, Tocqueville based the theory on his observation that in a free-market economy, the best and the brightest would quickly realize the real cash was in commerce, and choose their careers accordingly.

Almost 160 years later, Flex Crush put it another way:

"What's wrong with this picture?"

To wit:

• A former director of the CIA heads our government. He replaced an actor.

• Congress is made up of check-kiters, plagiarists, jokers who've memorized every word of *The Exorcist*, and guys who bear a striking resemblance to La-Z-Boy recliners.

• There's a fifty-three-year-old sitting on the Supreme Court who still lives with his mother.

"Congratulations, Foster. We're promoting you from smears and leaks to spins and distortions."

- NASA's idea of long-term planning is "What's for lunch?"
- The B-1 is a waste.
- The generals who supervise our weapons development seem to view their jobs as auditions for future employment with military contractors.
- A truly frightening number of former government officials have registered as foreign agents lobbying for Japan, including the current chairman of the Democratic Party, Ron Brown; former Senator Frank Church; former National security advisor, Richard V. Allen; ex-FCC chairman, Charles Ferris; former Assistant to President Carter, Stuart Eizenstat; and Vice President Bush's *Chief of Staff*, Retired Admiral Daniel J. Murphy.*
- And instead of "Do you promise to uphold the laws of the land?" the question—more often than not—seems to be "Do you swear to tell the truth, the whole truth, and nothing but the truth?"
- And the answer—more often than not—has become "I can't remember," "I don't recall," "I have no knowledge of that event," and "I have to check my diary."

"Whiners," said Flex. "Whiners with free postage."

Which may explain why, today, Real Men run for school board, not congress.

And why they don't check off the presidential campaign contribution on their tax returns. Anymore.

And why, given the choice, they wish there was a place on the ballot to vote for "none of the above."

And—perhaps most importantly—why they're in favor of term limits, and will vote for virtually anybody with a palpable measure of brain activity over an incumbent.

"Real Men are tired of electing people on the basis of eight-point-nine-second sound bites, and whether one candidate's commercials are more appealing—or

---

*For the full fifty-page list, see *Agents of Influence* by Pat Choate. (New York: Alfred A. Knopf, 1990.)

more appalling—than the stuff put into the other candidate's mouth by *his* image consultants," said Flex. "They're fed up with politicians who make up their minds on the basis of the latest public opinion polls; they're disgusted with professional hacks who've been running for office since the age of eighteen, and have never held a real job—or earned an honest day's pay—in their lives."

"Tough words there," I commented.

"Damn right," he replied. "But sometimes it just seems like there's nobody home in the government anymore. You can bang on the door of the Capitol, or the White House, and the lights are on, but there's just nobody home. Like the governor of New York: On one hand, he moans about the federal deficit and cutting the military budget—yet when the Pentagon says they *don't want* any more Grumman F-14's, he's the first to jump on a jet to Washington and scream that it's going to cost jobs in his state.

"A whiner runs to Washington; a Real Man would have grabbed the chairman of Grumman and said, "You knew this was coming. Why don't you start building things people *need*?"

"It's the same old story," Flex continued. "Everybody wants everything, and nobody's willing to sacrifice anything."

Flex stopped to catch his breath. (He had, after all, been talking faster than our beloved senators at a midnight session of Congress rushing through another pay raise.)

"Can't you think of *any*body you haven't mentioned who's a Real Man in the public sector today?" I asked.

Flex paused. He thought. "Barbara Jordan," he said at last. "Lloyd Bentsen. Thurgood Marshall and maybe . . ."

"What about Bill Clinton?"

Flex glared at me. He was incredulous. "Do you really have to ask?"

I shrugged.

Flex sighed, and looked out the window. He fiddled with a packet of Sweet N' Low.

"The problem isn't his sex life, or his draft defer- ments," Flex said. "Or even the way he whines on his saxophone. The problem is the way he whines in Real Life: He's been running for president since he was eighteen years old, yet he claims to be a political outsider. He whines about being misunderstood yet he can't seem to give a straight answer. He reminds me of somebody who claims to be a little pregnant."

"What do you mean?"

"Real Men inhale."

I had to concede Flex had a point. "Anybody else?" I asked.

"Yeah," he replied. "It's not on the same level, but you've got to give credit to the people who canceled the Sumitomo contract for subway cars in Los Angeles. It might not make a difference in the long run, but at least they took the position that if Southern Califor- nia industry can lead the world in Stealth bombers and satellites, surely they should be able to knock together something to get people from Long Beach to Glendale."

I nodded, and signaled for another cup of coffee.

"Look," Flex said finally, "Real Men don't belong to *any* political party today. They're tired of voting for the lesser of two evils. But they do know one thing: The Democrats will never win the White House again until they stop pandering to every special interest group, and dreaming about the fifteen million people on the left who *never* vote—and realize that it's the seven million in the middle who *do vote* that make the difference."

Flex paused.

"There are so many problems in this country," he said, shaking his head. "Somewhere we seem to have forgotten the basic premise of democracy: You can't make everybody happy. But you make choices for the *common good.*"

Perhaps.

But on the other hand, in this year of presidential elections, the following item may be the more timely issue:

Is George Bush a Real Man?

Alas, when it comes to "that masculinity thing," George Herbert Walker Bush is something of a quandary. Depending on where you stand, it could go either way. Consider:

Pro:	Con:
He's over six feet tall.	So was Willie Horton.
Not a liberal Democrat.	Real Men don't have 4 names.
Barbara.	Neil.
He's from Texas.	Not really.
Okay, he's actually from Maine.	Yeah, right next door to Sununu.
The Education President.	Right. Went to Yale.
Hunts and fishes.	In a cigarette boat.
The Environmental President.	How big is that cigarette boat?
"A thousand points of light."	Too bad they're fires in L.A.
Foreign policy expert.	Too bad L.A. wasn't in Russia.
He threw up on the *Japanese*!	He *threw up* on the Japanese!
Yeah? He was former head of the CIA.	Hey—Real Men are CIA operatives, not paper pushers.
Texas. Really. I swear, he's from Texas.	Right. Texas Avenue in Washington D.C.
Went to war in the Gulf.	Real Men finish what they start.

See? The arguments could go on endlessly.

(And in the case of the Gulf War, they may well go on endlessly. Yes, Real Men admire the Real Men and Real Women who served. But at the same time, they've begun to worry that this may go down in history as the war where Europe rented the United States' armed forces to kick Iraq out of Kuwait in order to protect Japanese oil supplies, which were ultimately used to destroy the American economy.)

But be that as it may, the question remains: Is George Bush a Real Man?

The answer is no.

And not because of the tube socks, his state visit to that strange and alien foreign country known as "the supermarket," or even the way he drops his g's and puts on an "aw, shucks" accent when he drops in for a photo opportunity with the little people who elected him in the first place.

No. The real reason is much more fundamental.

No matter if you're a Democrat or a Republican, in the entire history of the country—no, make that the entire history of civilized thought—can you imagine *any* list, in *any* category, that would include Dan Quayle, Clarence Thomas, and David Souter as—in George Bush's own words—"The best men for the job"?

9

Sixty Seconds to a More Manly Vocabulary

*R*eal Men speak in clear, concise sentences. As in, "Pull it over." "Drop the gun." And "Watch it—my friend has a video camera recording everything."

With this in mind:

- Real Men never begin any question with the phrase "Did there come a time..."
- Real Men do not say "Thank you for sharing."
- Real Men understand that anyone who boasts (usually after an insult) "I tell the truth," never is.
- And Real Men don't "vet" anything, unless it walks on four legs.
- Among Real Men, "boomers" are nuclear submarines.
- "Outing" is an activity that involves sleeping bags and a Coleman lantern.
- "Networking" is the act of switching from CBS to NBC.
- An "empowerment" is something you do with an orange extension cord.
- Real Men do not ♡ anything.
- They don't use the words "adult child," "inner child," "infotainment," or "shopaholic."

- Real Men have learned that anything referred to as "the cutting edge," usually isn't.
- And that when a piece of art, a film, or a negotiating style is hailed as being "in your face," Real Men know the other applicable synonyms are "obnoxious," "arrogant," "bombastic," and "ultimately irrelevant."
- Real Men do not "dissemble," "obfuscate," or "deconstruct." (And for those academics among us who earn their salaries "deconstructing literature"— that is, the act of ignoring what someone actually wrote, and postulating what they meant to write, let's deconstruct the word "deconstruct": "To rip down, destroy, or demolish." Which may explain why Real Men teach biology.)
- The word "dude" does not appear in the Real Man's linguistic pantheon, unless it's followed immediately by "ranch."
- Real Men never say "Let's cut to the chase."
- Or "How special."
- Or "What's the bottom line?"
- Nor do they use the phrases "it's hip," "it's hot," "it's trendy," "it's happening"—or any combination of *any* of the above. (Real Men are on the next jet out when somebody says, "Let's cut to the bottom line here. Is it hip, hot, trendy, and happening?")
- And perhaps most important, Real Men do not litter their conversation with the word "thing," as in:

> "That wimp thing."
> "That domestic thing."
> And especially "How the hell am I going to win this election thing?"

The Real Men Industries, Inc.
Annual Report
for 1993

REAL MEN INDUSTRIES, INC.
1 Big Picture Road
Corporate Park, Texas

January 1993

Dear Man:

Well, another year has gone by. And as we all know, it's never been harder to walk like a man, talk like a man, or cut down on the paperwork.

(And am I the only one who's noticed that the so-called computerized paperless office seems to create polar ice sheets of paper?)

Nevertheless, the two basic credos of Real Men in business remain intact:

1. You *can't* make millions in real estate foreclosure.

2. "I *earned* the mileage awards. I had to sit on the plane."

In other news, here are today's Real Men in Business:

• *Robert Crandall*, CEO of American Airlines, for running one of the only national, eastern, western, continental, pan-American and trans-world airlines that hasn't flown off into bankruptcy.
• *Ross Perot*, founder of Electronic Data Services, corporate commando, and provider of the Real Man quote of the year: "At EDS, we had a rule that the first one who sees a snake kills it. At General Motors, the first thing they do is form a committee on snakes."
• *And a posthumous acknowledgment to Sam Walton,*

for building the Real Man's idea of a corner grocery store, Wal-Mart.

Then there are the corporations and individuals who no longer represent the Real Man's Ideal in business:

• *Carl Icahn*. Real Men don't take $469 million out of the company, and let TWA go bankrupt.

• *IBM*, the company that all but invented the computer, for blowing the market in laptops to Toshiba. (IBM's motto seems to have changed from "Think" to "Think about Reorganizing Again." No wonder it's called "Big Blue.")

• *American Express*, for commercials that seem designed to convince us that *we don't even want to know anybody* who carries an American Express Card. (Remember the spot with the eighteen yuppies gorging themselves at what appears to be a business dinner in a restaurant? The one where the guy worries about the bill, and then says something like, "No problem. I've got an American Express card, so I order another bottle of wine." Wrong. A Real Man would have been thinking, "Why the hell didn't I have this in the conference room, and order in Popeye's fried chicken?")

• *Lee Iacocca*. (Lido, Lido...Yes, the Japanese are unfair. Yes, they're predatory, biased, and self-protectionist. But Lido: have you *driven* a Honda lately? Give us a call afterwards, and we'll talk.)

• And GM, for five reasons:

1. Great Moments in Compassionate Public Relations: For announcing the week before Christmas of 1991 that 71,000 jobs and 21 plants would be cut—but not specifying who, what, or when the changes would take place. "Ho, ho, ho. And a merry Christmas to you, too."

2. The "Henry Ford, You Can Have Any Color So Long as It's Black Citation" for ignoring the fact that an *entire generation* of Americans loves the way Nissans, Toyotas, and BMWs feel—while GM seems to have taken the position that "one day those people are going to grow up and *want* to own cars that drive like waterbeds."

3. The "We Care About Our Environment Award" for continuing to kick and scream "It's impossible" every time the government wants to tighten emission controls and raise gas mileage standards, while the Japanese just shrug and say "No Problem."

4. The "Customer Comes First Trophy" for low-balling customers with stripped cars, and then tacking on exorbitant charges for everything from glove compartment lights to real spare tires, ensuring that in the "Places I Most Look Forward to Visiting" category, a Chevy dealership ranks right below Cambodia.

5. The "Rube Goldberg Prize for Intelligent Design," for continually advertising "radically redesigned dashboards" every year, only confirming for many people that after seventy-five years in the automotive business, GM still hasn't figured out where to put the radio.

In other business news, there are three final points:

1. Once again this year, Real Men won't be applying for the Baldrige Quality Award for the Management of American Business. Why not? If you've got the free time, the extra manpower, and the loose change to hire the consultants, spend a year in meetings, and fill out the eight-hundred-page application, it shouldn't take a contest to figure out what's wrong with your management.

2. It's been noted that while America bought some forty-two million computers between 1980 and 1990, there was no corresponding increase in productivity. Why? Real Men suspect that whatever time was saved with the computers went into making graphs and charts. We don't make decisions anymore—we make visuals. And too many of them are all but incomprehensible. (Real Men wonder: Can anyone pinpoint the exact moment in the early nineties when American business seemed to embrace the credo that "Bad news always looks better in a pie chart"?)

3. And finally, you'll be pleased to know Real Men Industries has rejected the advice of our (now) former corporate image firm, and *will not* be changing our motto to: "Serving Personkind and the Environment since 400 B.C."

Enjoy the rest of the annual report.

Flex Crush

Flex Crush, CEO
Real Men Industries

REAL MEN: A VANISHING COMMODITY

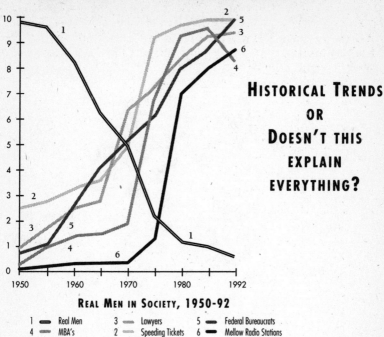

HISTORICAL TRENDS OR DOESN'T THIS EXPLAIN EVERYTHING?

REAL MEN IN SOCIETY, 1950-92

1 Real Men   3 Lawyers   5 Federal Bureaucrats
4 MBA's   2 Speeding Tickets   6 Mellow Radio Stations

CURRENT GREAT LIES OF AMERICAN BUSINESS
(NEVER USED BY REAL MEN)

CREDIBILITY PROBLEMS

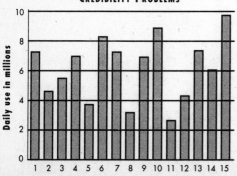

1. "I wanted to, but the boss wouldn't go for it."
2. "I left the message on E-Mail."
3. "Think of it as a chance to start over."
4. "We're *all* going to share in the hardship."
5. "It hurts more because I like you so much."
6. "I think of us as a team."
7. "Synergy."
8. "It's just an exercise. Nothing is written in stone."
9. "Let's leave the fine points to the lawyers."
10. "I like to get the feel of things before I make changes."
11. "*I* don't care, but my lawyer insists on it."
12. "Your fax must be broken."
13. "It's a prototype. The bugs'll be out before production."
14. "Just a tiny point or two in the contract and we're done."
15. "I don't care about short-term."

WHERE THE TIME GOES
HOW THE REAL MAN WOULD LIKE TO SPEND HIS BUSINESS DAY

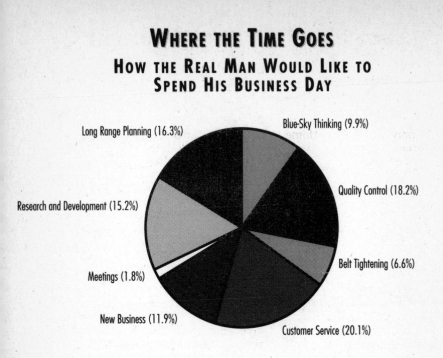

Long Range Planning (16.3%)

Blue-Sky Thinking (9.9%)

Quality Control (18.2%)

Research and Development (15.2%)

Belt Tightening (6.6%)

Meetings (1.8%)

New Business (11.9%)

Customer Service (20.1%)

HOW HE ACTUALLY DOES

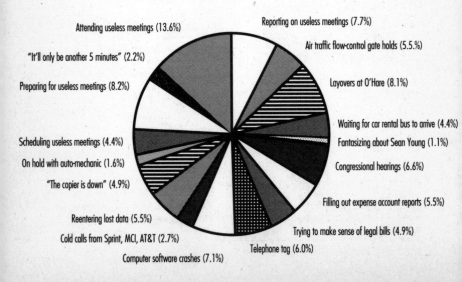

Attending useless meetings (13.6%)

Reporting on useless meetings (7.7%)

Air traffic flow-control gate holds (5.5.%)

"It'll only be another 5 minutes" (2.2%)

Layovers at O'Hare (8.1%)

Preparing for useless meetings (8.2%)

Waiting for car rental bus to arrive (4.4%)

Fantasizing about Sean Young (1.1%)

Scheduling useless meetings (4.4%)

Congressional hearings (6.6%)

On hold with auto-mechanic (1.6%)

"The copier is down" (4.9%)

Filling out expense account reports (5.5%)

Reentering lost data (5.5%)

Cold calls from Sprint, MCI, AT&T (2.7%)

Trying to make sense of legal bills (4.9%)

Telephone tag (6.0%)

Computer software crashes (7.1%)

Real Man Corporations
(And Other Real Man Assets)

Boeing	Harley Davidson	Nucor Steel
John Deere	Intel	Black & Decker
The USS *Nimitz*	Federal Express	Chicago
Agway	Home Depot	Lands' End
Texas	The C-5A	Toys R' Us
Levi-Strauss	Canada*	Jack Welch
Johnson & Johnson	Stanley Tools	Submarines
The Cont'ntl Shelf	The Cont'ntl Divide	Motorola
Route 80	Warren Buffet	David and Harry
Wal-Mart	Saturn (the planet)	Hewlett-Packard
Saint Louis	The Price Club	McDonald's
Thomas Watson, Jr.	American Airlines	3M
UPS	MicroSoft	Dell Computer
Ralph Nader	George Lucas	The Clydesdales
	Ford Rouge, Dearborn	

(*Less Quebec)

Whiners

GM	Exxon	IBM
Sears	Dow-Corning	Victor Kiam

Other Major Liabilities

Exorbitant hotel room telephone charges

Abusive pay-phone long-distance charges

Teenagers with beepers

Stapleton International Airport

Atlantic City

Anybody who says, "Sue me. I have deeper pockets than you do."

Phone calls that begin, "Can you hold for Mr./Mrs. Smith?"

Outplacement services

Stock market newsletters

Commercials that end, "We thought you'd like to know."

Real Man Jobs for the Nineties

Owner of Jiffy Lube vs. Slick PR guy

Commodities Grower vs. Commodities Trader

Pawn Shop Owner vs. Arbitrageur

Welder

Teacher

Roofer

Stonemason

Father

President of Byelorussia

"To hell with finding my masculinity. The only thing
I want to find is the guy who sold me
Amalgamated Sludge at 63¼."

PART II
The Real Man at Play

Real Man Quiz #3

Q: What does a Real Man use a wok for?

A: Oil changes.

Q: Where does a Real Man get his hair cut?

A: Home Depot.

11
Sports

R eal Men "communicate" on hockey rinks.
They "discuss things" at the fifty-yard line.
The Real Man's idea of an "encounter ses-
sion" is two guys squaring off at center ring, Caesars,
Vegas.

Yes, as we all know, sports are the Real Man's
favorite pastime. (Okay. I stand corrected. They're
actually number two, but you can't get number one
twenty-four hours a day on ESPN.)

Sadly enough though, even major league sports
—that ideal we hold so dearly, that thing which
gives us something to do on Saturday afternoon,
Sunday afternoon, and Monday Nights—that spirit
of competition that has such a grip on our hearts
and wallets thanks to the office betting pool—yes,
even professional sports, which should be the final bastion of Real Men, has become a bistro for
whiners.

"Every season it's the same old story," said Flex.
"Players whining about salaries. Coaches whining about
players. Owners whining about everything the coaches
and players forgot to whine about.

"He says if you don't give him something to hit,
he's going to buy the team and put you
on the ground crew."

"And what's responsible for this?" he asked. "What plague has descended upon the house of Ruth, the gridiron of Unitas, the playing fields of Willis Reed, Walt Frazier and Gordie Howe?

"Sports agents," he said. "Locusts from hell in Gucci loafers.

"It used to be that people played for the love of the game," Flex explained. "The action, the color, the fans. The idea that anything is possible on one perfect afternoon.

"But not anymore. We don't reward excellence these days; we bribe for mediocrity. We've got .229 hitters, and pitchers with 12-12 years and a 4.12 ERA earning millions. Guys who can't make a jump-shot on an eight-foot basket earning a million six. Players with four-year contracts that rival the operating budget of Istanbul complaining about their hotel rooms.

"Now mind you—I'm not saying that Wade Boggs should go to bed hungry at night, even if it might help. Or that Barry Bonds should be forced to stay at the Y—even if *that* might help.

"But it's more than just the money. It's the attitude. The idea that the only color that counts these days is Federal Green."

Flex paused.

"At the rate things are going, we're going to need an entirely new way to keep score in the nineties: The Earned Riches Average. Bank-Tending penalties. Shots on Management. A Designated Field Agent. A fifteen-yard setback for too many men in Municipals. And forget about the coin toss: that's chump change these days. If they wanted to be realistic, they oughta be flipping T-Bills out there.

"All I know is one thing," Flex added. "Sometime in the next few years, I'm going to be watching a football game, and the ref is going to stop the clock,

booming: 'Time Out. Indianapolis. Number 29. Dick-
erson. Contract Renegotiation.'"

Well . . . Like the best sports fans, Flex was not exactly without his opinions. But to paraphrase every
local sportscaster who's ever had the honor to sit
next to the Asian Female news co-anchor at 11:00,
"Let's go to the prose."

Real Men in sports don't hold out, show up late for
training, or refuse to sign autographs for kids.

They don't earn over a million dollars a year and
gripe about not being appreciated.

They don't get busted six times for drugs, and then
blame the problem on society.

And Real Men in sports don't demand contracts
that require they be "one of the four highest paid
players in the NBA," regardless of their performance
on the court. (Real Men have some perspective about
the money. They don't demand more than they're
worth. And if all else fails, they're always vindicated in
arbitration.)

Real Men in sports don't write their autobiogra-
phies when they're only thirty-one; they don't demand that other players be booted from the team;
they don't hold themselves up as "models for youth,"
and drop $70,000 betting on golf matches.

Real Men don't play the game as if they're "for
rent"; they're loyal to the cities that support them.

In the owners category, Real Owners don't second-
guess their staff and players. They don't meddle.
They pay fairly. And they, too, are loyal to the fans:
They don't cater only to the guys in the skyboxes,
and threaten to move the team if things aren't going
their way.

And as far as coaches or managers go, there's
only one hard and fast rule: Real Men don't advertise
Slim-Fast.

So who are the Real Men in sports?

Eddie Murray of the Mets; Robert Parish of the Celtics; Ronnie Lott of the Raiders.

They show up, they do the job.

Just like Bruce Smith (the Buffalo defensive end), Larry Bird, Cal Ripken, Dave Winfield, and—although he's not playing anymore—Bo Jackson. (That's one other thing Bo knows about: Being a Man.)

Phil Simms and Dan Marino are both Real Men—especially when compared to the now-retired Brian Bosworth. (Real Men plan for the next game—not a movie career.)

Andre Dawson is obviously a Real Man. (Real Men loved it when Dawson paid the $1000 fine for disputing a strike call by umpire Joe West, and wrote on the memo line of the check "Donation for the Blind.")

Real Men admire Jim Palmer for giving it one last shot; they look up to hockey goalie Ray LeBlanc and power hitter Cecil Fielder for never giving up.

Real Men play in the Pacific Division of the NBA. They're on defense in the NFL. And they're usually in the penalty box in the National Hockey League.

Real Men produce when it counts; they earn the money.

It's the spirit of the Celtics, the Islanders, and the Chicago Bears. (Especially the Bears: You have to be a Real Man to believe in a running quarterback.)

It's the work ethic of the Washington Redskins. (And before we get into some kind of politically correct brawl here, let's deal with the issue of team nicknames once and for all: Yes, dropping the phrase "Redskins" might be considered giving in to the whiners. But on the other hand, it's just not worth arguing about—especially when there are so many bigger battles to fight, like ticket prices. In the end, Real Men don't care what the name is changed to—so long as it isn't the "Seattle Sushi." And

God help us all if the Green Bay meat-packers ever organize.)

Among the coaches and owners, Bill Walsh, Pat Riley, and Jerry West are all Real Men, along with Jerry Glanville of the Falcons. (Real Men, after all, *do* leave tickets for Elvis.) But on the other hand, Robert and James Irsay of the Colts are major-league whiners: Real Men don't sneak the team from Baltimore to Indianapolis in the middle of the night.

Obviously, this discussion could go on. But as all Real Men love stats, here's the box score:

Real Men in Sports

Andre Dawson	Howard Johnson	Ray LeBlanc
Kirby Puckett	Whitey Herzog	The Celtics
The 1991 World Series	Nolan Ryan	Jim McMahon
Sparky Anderson	Robin Yount	George Brett
Jim Abbott	Matt Millen	Chris Mullin
George Foreman	Jim Kelley	The PGA Seniors
	Marcus Allen	
	Frank Deford, and the National	

Whiners

Darryl Strawberry	Martina Navratilova	Lew Holtz
The Dodgers	The Lakers	The Rams
Mark Rypien	Lawrence Taylor	Benito Santiago
Steve Garvey	Charles Barkley	Wally Joyner
Gregg Jefferies	Patrick Ewing	Kevin Mitchell
Jack Clark	Benoit Benjamin	Jose Canseco
Steve Sax	Wade Boggs	Georgia Frontiere

Of course, no discussion of major-league sports would be complete without a discussion of major-league sports fans.

Real Men sit in the rafters—not in the "all expenses

paid," "bring me some more chardonnay," "don't the players look cute down there, honey," sky boxes.

Real Men have season tickets, and show up for every game.

Real Men are fans through good and bad; they don't suddenly discover "their team" when it's in a title race.

Real Men don't believe that dumping beer on the outfielders is necessarily the most effective form of constructive criticism.

And when it comes to the gamesite, Real Men are still purists: The only amenities they require are hot dogs, real grass, and weather. Real Men, after all, aren't interested in having a shopping mall attached to their sports facilities; Real Men don't mind sitting in the cold in Giants Stadium.*

At home, Real Men will watch virtually anything that glows on ESPN—although they still can't quite understand the appeal of synchronized swimming.

Real Men admire the Real Men announcers: Vin Scully, Ahmad Rashad, Chris Berman, Nick Charles, Fred Hickman, John Sanders, Terry Bradshaw, Ernie Harwell, Chick Hearn, Johnny Most, Harry Caray, John Madden, and Pat Summeral. ("Hey—any guy who sells hammers in the off hours can't be all bad," said Flex.)

Plus Frank Gifford. ("Sure they rag on him, but he does the job—with grace.")

And finally, Real Men still love the Super Bowl— although they've begun to worry that the "National Corporate High Holy Day" has become a little overblown, and wonder if it really needs to be ninety-four

---

*Speaking of which, Flex used this as an opportunity to explain why he's certain that Jimmy Hoffa is—in fact—buried in the end zone of Giants Stadium. "It's obvious," Flex remarked. "After the two goons whacked him, I'm sure they went to the boss and asked, 'So what should we do with him now?' And I'm willing to bet the guy said, 'I don't give a damn. Plant him in the fucking end zone.' And goons being goons, I'm sure that's exactly what they did."

hours long, not counting the Super Bowl eve gala, the three pregame and two postgame shows, including the "up close and personal" interview with the guy who lives next door to a guy who knows somebody who almost got the job driving the losing team's bus.

"That's all well and good," I said to Flex, "but if you had to pick one person—one shining example that represents the very best of Real Men in sports—who would it be?"

"That's easy," he replied. "Cubs fans."

12

The Real Man and Television

Tonight's question, students of Real Manhood, is the following:

What is the single most important invention (for men, that is) of the twentieth century?

Minoxidil? Exit ramps? A pair of Merc 420 outboards? No. The answer is remote control.

Why?

Because with the advent of remote control, the last great sport of the twentieth century was invented: Video Surfing.

The fine and practiced art of spending hours in front of the television set, skimming from channel to channel, watching sixty-three shows at once, never having to witness a single commercial, or miss a second of the all-important fifty-sixth-minute climax when Jack Lord *gets his man*.

(Admittedly, this is bad news for the networks and their advertisers. But as every Real Man knows, it's the deep dark secret of the Nielsen ratings: Thanks to video surfing—or "zapping" as the nonenlightened call it—nobody is really watching *anything* all the way through anymore.)

Yes, thanks to the miracle of video surfing, Real Men were able to avoid large chunks of "thirtysomething" at will. (And let's be truthful here: Real Men did not "share an aching communal sense of loss" when "thirtysomething" got axed from the schedule. First, because Real Men require capital letters. And second, because Real Men felt that what Michael—Mr. Angst—really needed was for somebody to give him a good smack in the mouth, and to say, "Snap out of it, pal.")

With video surfing, Real Men can start out with Jay Leno's monologue, switch over to Arsenio, and then rebound to Dave, all without missing a single instance of the spontaneous "Really? You brought a clip?" dialogue/interchange.

You don't have to miss a second of the riveting fly-fishing action on "Bassmasters."

Or a moment of Vince McMahon and any of his World Wrestling Federation's "Steel-Cage Tag-Team Death Matches." (And while it's true that Real Men see these bouts as a grand metaphor in opposition to the stifling rituals of postindustrialist society, vis-à-vis men and their relationship to corporate culture in a society that's chosen to ignore its rich and nurturing heritage of mythopoetic traditions—go ahead, read it again—the *real* reason we love wrestling is for the locker room interviews. Example: "Well, Vince, I just want my fans to know that if I should lose to Dr. Death at the Hartford Civic Arena on January fifth, tickets fifteen, twenty, and twenty-five dollars, available through Ticketron, with plenty of good seats still available—I promise that at our long-awaited rematch on January eighteenth at the Philadelphia Spectrum—tickets fifteen, twenty, and twenty-five dollars, available at the box office, or through Ticketmaster—I swear Vince, I will kill him.")

With video surfing, Real Men can catch all the Real Men on television: Barry Corbin, Charles Dutton, Tim Matheson, Ken Wahl, Corbin Bernsen, Larry King, Tom Selleck, and "Rat Patrol"—and not only *all at the same time*, but with the added benefit of driving unwanted in-laws, process servers, spouses (spices?), and even hyperactive children *right out of the room*.

You can spend months without hearing a single celebrity say, "Sure, I'm rich, I'm famous, I date beautiful women . . . but nobody knows the real me." Or be subjected to interviews that begin, "Since I got out of the Betty Ford clinic . . ." And never once do you have to hear the words "I took this role because it was a stretch," or "The only reason I posed in *Playboy* was because I wanted to . . ."—and here's where you begin to reach for the remote control— ". . . send a message to women that they should be proud of their bodies." Sure, honey.

But wait—as they say on every late night commercial— there's more:

You can surf from Norm Abram on the "Yankee Workshop" (he's what every Real Man aspires to be around the house—even if we can't figure out what the hell a "dado" is), cut back over to Justin Wilson on "Louisiana Cookin'" (Real Man? In his own words, "I gar-run-*tee it*"), then do a risky triple axel around the dial to Mutual of Omaha's Jim Fowler (it's about time he got promoted beyond the role of "Let's watch as Jim hops out of the boat into the typhoid-ridden swamp to show us the razor-sharp six-inch teeth of the carnivorous Floridian alligator"), and finally, shoot right, right through the culture pipeline to catch Bob Vila, star of the seminal version of "This Old House." (Real Men miss Bob. They dream of visiting him at home while he's cooking breakfast, and tapping him on the shoulder: "Hey Bob, what're you doing there?" "Makin' eggs." "Hmmm. Looks interesting. Mind if I try?")

Plus, you'll never miss *any* of the good stuff on the Home Shopping Network. (Yes, Real Men *do* order from HSN. "Where else can you buy magnesium socket wrenches at three-thirty in the morning?" Flex said. "*That's* what makes America great.")

And equally important, utilizing the same degree of precision hand-eye coordination that's made him King of the Road, a skillful Real Man can skim through an entire evening of "dramatic reenactments," and news reporters pounding on doors saying, "I'm sorry to tell you that your husband just died in a plane crash. So how do you feel?"—*without once* feeling like you want to get up from the set and take a shower.

Of course, there are other shows—whiner shows—that Real Men don't watch. And the full list follows on the next page.

But after millions of hours surfing on the video waves, Real Men have come to two irrefutable conclusions about the electron box:

1. There are no amazing discoveries on "Amazing Discoveries." And,

2. Fox TV's dating program, "Studs," and CNN's "Crossfire" (with Michael Kinsley and Pat Buchanan), are actually the same show: a bunch of people sitting around talking about how much they'd like to screw each other.

The Real Man's

	SUNDAY	MONDAY	TUESDAY
4:00	**PGA Golf** from Japanese-owned Pebble Beach w/ Bryant Gumbel	**Oprah:** Women who hate men.	**Phil:** Men who love women who hate men.
5:00		**A Current Affair:** Women who slept with JFK	**Hard Copy:** Women who slept with JFK and Geraldo
6:00	**PBS Spotlight:** Oliver Stone on the sixties.	**Maude**	**Cagney and Lacey**
		Get a Life	
7:00	**Amazing Discoveries:** 1,000-Year Shoelaces (2 hrs.)	**C-Span:** "Don't Blame Me": Profiles of Congress.	**thirtysomething:** the reunion.
8:00			
9:00	MOW: **Rock-a-Bye Baby:** Valerie Bertinelli as an abused wife forced to kill her husband to get her children back.	MOW: **On the Tree Tops:** Donna Mills as an abused wife who must kick drugs and kill her husband to get her kids back.	MOW: **When the Wind Blows:** Victoria Principal as an abused wife who must kill her husband during a hurricane to get her kids back.
10:00			
11:00	Cher sells something.	**Dave Del Dotto:** Foreclose on your best friends' house to riches.	Cher sells something else.
12:00			

Television Hell

WEDNESDAY	THURSDAY	FRIDAY	SATURDAY
Sally: Cross-dressers who hate men who love women who hate men.	**Maury:** Women who love cross-dressers who hate men who love women who hate men who love women who are addicted to Oprah, Sally, and Phil.	**Geraldo:** Women I've slept with.	**MTV News:** A new Michael Jackson video. (1 hr.)
Now It Can Be Told: More women I've slept with.		**Attitudes:** Swimwear for the "Larger Woman"	**MTV:** The Making of the video. (1 hr.) **MTV:** The Michael Jackson interview about the new video. (1 hr.) **The video.** (:09)
Home Shopping Network Special: Ten Years of Salad Shooter			
Prime-Time Live: Diane interviews Sting about the rain forest.	Highlights of the Democratic National Convention (3 hrs.)	Highlights of the Republican National Convention (3 hrs.)	**Democratic Response:** House Speaker Tom Foley's reply to the new Michael Jackson video. (:90)
MOW: **The Cradle Will Rock:** Veronica Hamel as an abused wife with an eating disorder who must kill her husband to get her kids back.	MOW: **When the Bough Breaks:** Mel Harris as an abused wife who must fight cancer and kill her husband to get her kids back.	MOW: **The Cradle Will Fall:** Stefanie Powers as an abused wife who must overcome amnesia and kill her husband to get her kids back.	MOW: **And Down Will Come Baby:** Jaclyn Smith as an abused wife who must go to Europe to kill her husband and get her kids back.
HBO Special: Comics complain about dating and life in L.A.	**Glorious Infidels:** Iraqi TV. (Leased programming)		MOW: **Cradle and All:** Jane Seymour as an abused wife who must sneak behind Nazi lines to kill her husband and get her kids back.

13

The Real Man's Guide to Periodical (and Other) Literature

Contrary to popular belief, Real Men read.
They read spreadsheets, they read blueprints,
they read the entire federal tax code.

For fun.

What don't Real Men read?

Instruction manuals, roadmaps, speedometers,
letters from Ed McMahon, anything marked "Final
Notice," most traffic signs, and all books with titles
like *Love's Heaving Breast.*

Real Men don't read the *Sun,* the *Star,* the *Enquirer,*
or any other publication that claims to have exclusive
pictures of Elvis having sex with one of Bill Clinton's
old girlfriends at a Motel Six. On Mars.

For sheer pleasure and relaxation—light reading,
that is—Real Men subscribe to the following publica-
tions, all of which actually exist:

Jane's Defense Weekly
The Bulletin of the Atomic Scientists
Meat Plant Management
Collision and Tow Age
Dismantler's Digest
The Journal of Air Traffic Control

"The final message seems to be 'Hey, no problem—
nothing's written in stone.'"

*Moody's Bond Survey
The Auto and Flat-Glass Journal
Minnesota Smoke Eater
The Iron Worker
National Certified Public Accountant
Experimental Neurology
Wyoming Beverage Analyst
National Sheriff
Pennsylvania Highway Builder
Illinois Master Plumber
Iowa Pork Producer
Meat & Poultry
Doors & Windows
Walls & Ceilings
Rubber & Plastics
Pit & Quarry
Implement & Tractor
Hydraulics & Pneumatics
Earthquakes & Volcanoes*
and
Garbage, the Practical Journal for the Environment.

Of course, not all the reading Real Men partake in is done solely for pleasure.

And when Real Men seek a deeper understanding of the world around them—when they require a cool, hard-eyed professional assessment of politics, or of the morass that surrounds us in our daily lives, Real Men know there are always two writers they can turn to who will provide wisdom, clarity, and a concise and truthful analysis of the human condition:

Stephen King and Tom Clancy.

Both "big picture" guys.

But in case you're one of the two, or perhaps three, Real Men on the planet who haven't read King or Clancy, here's a summary of everything they've ever written:

Chapter Six
Monday, the Worst Day

Aboard the USS Dallas

The world was ending.

Jack Ryan had been awake—what was it now—two thousand straight hours? He'd gotten up that morning in Morrow, England, where he worked as a data analyst for the CIA, and after reaching his conclusion—a calculated guess, actually, but that's what he was paid for—he took a British Harrier jet from the HMS *Invincible* to Loring Air Force Base in Maine, where he switched to an F-15 Eagle, and flew south to Andrews Air Force Base at Mach 2, where he was met by a marine sergeant with a navy-gray Chevy who drove him up the George Washington Parkway to CIA headquarters at Langley, Virginia, where he was ushered into the oak-paneled office of the DCI—director of Central Intelligence—who conferred with COMSUBLANT—the navy's commander of submarine forces in the Atlantic—who, in turn, met with the president in the lead-lined NSA situation room beneath the White House on Pennsylvania Avenue—and then issued a FLASH signal on the SSIX—the submarine satellite information exchange, via a naval communications satellite locked in a geosynchronous orbit 24,000 miles above the earth. And now, after a brief but bumpy trip out on a Super Stallion helicopter, Ryan was standing in the control room of the USS *Dallas*, a 688-class U.S. nuclear attack boat, 2,000 feet below the Atlantic, just under the thermocline, 120 nautical miles north of Bermuda—in that area otherwise known as the Bermuda Triangle.

"I've got to get out of here," Ryan all but screamed to himself. At least he wanted to scream, but the words wouldn't come. The walls were closing in on him. Claustrophobia. Seasickness. He was turning green. Was that condensation on the pipes, or blood? In the pit of his stomach he had that churning feeling—and *what about* that "cook" with the nineteen-inch meat cleaver? The pressure was getting to him. He knew what Evil was out there—or at least he thought he knew—a horrible, black void, sucking at the life force of the world.

"Coffee, Jack?" Captain Puris was one of the best boat drivers in the U.S. Navy. Annapolis. Stanford. Family man. Played some ball at Notre Dame. He could be kind, he could be tough. The enlisted men loved him. He was all things to all people. A good man.

"Sure," said Jack. But what if he was wrong, he thought to himself. What if it was just another piece of disinformation by renegade KGB agents? Or the Black September Group? Or Mossad, the GUI, Iraqi fanatics, and the Colombians, all working in league with our own free-lance operatives?

"Contact, bearing zero-zero-four," first-class sonarman Martin Luther King Clinton called out from the sonar room. He was a good man.

"Do we have an identification on the contact?" Puris asked.

"I'm not sure, sir," Clinton replied. Sweat poured off his brow. Panic seized his throat. He wasn't sure what was out there—but every cell in his body, every experience in his all-too-short life told him one thing: Whatever you do, *don't open the torpedo tube doors*. Get a grip on yourself, he thought. He spoke calmly: "I think it's some kind of unspeakable Evil that's sucking at the life force of the world." It was a good guess.

"Range six thousand," executive officer Ammiratti replied. It was a good range. First class fire controlman Cosmopulos was feeding data from the target motion analyzer to the Mark 117 fire control computer. It was a good computer. The diving officer, O'Harah, leveled the boat. It was a good move. They were all good men.

"Match bearings and shoot," Puris cried out, and the two MK-48 torpedoes were in the water. They were good torpedoes.

"They're pinging her, sir."

Yes, whatever Evil was out there, it was nothing that a good cup of coffee, a few good American men, and a couple trillion dollars of U.S. military hardware couldn't take care of.

"Coffee, sir?"

Jack took the saucer from the cook, First Mate Juan Jesus Cortez. He was a good man, too—even if he *was* psychotically attached to the meat cleaver.

Jack sipped the coffee.

He was going to save the world.

14

A Few Notes on Music

As every Real Man knows, you can't spackle, paint, sandblast, top out a skyscraper, pour cement, drive, operate heavy machinery, have sex, or put in a decent set of shocks without the proper musical accompaniment.

(After writing that paragraph, I realize that for a small faction of Real Men, the concepts of "operating heavy machinery" and "having sex" are often the same thing. *Wrong*. Real Men don't brag about *that*. But as I said, we were talking about a small faction here.)

Still, the subject at hand is the man, and his music.

Real Men will listen to anything by the Boss, the Chairman, the Count, the Queen of Soul, Queen Latifah, Prince, Duke Ellington, the Hardest-Working Man in Show Business, the man in the Black Hat, Roy Orbison, and all of the Kings: Nat, Ben E., and Elvis.

(And although no one's exactly sure why so many corporate and aristocratic titles have been assumed by musicians, it may have something to do with the Real Man's Basic Rules of Nomenclature: Never play poker with a guy named Doc; never pick a fight with somebody named Tiny; and never, ever hire a band fronted by a guy named Moose.)

Getting back to music, today most Real Men own CD players—but they miss the album covers, and *still buy* all their music on cassette. ("Seven ninety-nine for a cassette with one good song is pushing it," said Flex. "But fourteen bucks is practically a down payment on an office building in Houston.")

Real Men would like to hear more new music—but can't seem to find radio stations that play any. ("I refuse to believe anybody calls up and actually asks to hear 'Muskrat Love,'" Flex remarked. "And it's not that I don't like Phil Collins. I do. He doesn't pretend he's eighteen years old. But the people who are programming radio stations seem so narrow-minded I'm afraid that I'm going riding down the highway one day, and punch in K-SAFE Radio: 'All Phil Collins, All Whitney Houston, All the Time.')

A frightening thought, indeed.

Real Men love all the old Motown, doo-wop, blues, and rock and roll songs that evoke especially cherished memories—like the first time they had sex (with a partner, that is), or the first night they got blindingly stupid drunk. (Again, these two are often one and the same.) But Real Men wince every time one of those old songs is co-opted for a bank, car, or credit card commercial. ("I swear," said Flex. "I commit suicide the day the Rolling Stone's 'Tumbling Dice' shows up in an ad for a Trump casino. What's next? 'White Rabbit' for Volkswagen? 'When I'm Sixty-four' for Blue Cross? 'The Bitch is Back' for Leona Helmsley's hotels? Is nothing in this world sacred anymore?")

And speaking of the World's Greatest Rock and Roll Band, Real Men still adore the Rolling Stones, although they wonder if Mick Jagger—at fifty—isn't pushing the outer limits on the suitability of Spandex for businesswear. (And in much the same vein, Real Men have some advice for Rod Stewart: Get a haircut, and stop singing about high school.)

Real Men admire all the Real Men rock and rollers who have managed to age gracefully: Van Morrison, Clapton, Harrison, Cocker, Dylan, Bob Seger, the Grateful Dead, and (honorary mention) James Taylor. (Plus Keith Richards, a man who stands in living defiance of most insurance company actuarial tables.)

And although Real Men don't have a problem with rap, they do have a problem with people who want to put warning stickers on albums, and warn that inner-city music will lead to the end of American society as we now know it. (Real Men wonder exactly what country these people—these fifty-year-olds—were living in when they were twenty-three years old, in 1965. "I know the answer to that one," Flex interjected. "They were touring Disneyland with the New Christy Minstrels, waiting for 'Muskrat Love' to come out.")

And while all Real Men have put in their time watching the girls in lingerie on MTV, Real Men have come to realize that virtually any idiot with a video camera can re-create the three shots it takes to produce a "classic" rock video: 1) A wide shot of the band onstage, with lots of smoke, explosions, and strobe lights; 2) a close-up of the blonde in the front row (lingerie optional), amidst the throngs of screaming fans who are holding up matches; and 3) a long shot of the lead singer and the blonde driving down a deserted highway in the American Southwest, in a fifties convertible. (Lingerie mandatory.)

So what don't Real Men listen to?

George Michael complaining about being famous; rock stars lecturing about politics; Madonna revealing still more about her life (thank you, but we've all heard enough), and Michael Bolton, period. ("He's so over the top," said Flex. "Mister Emotion. Mr. King of Pain. Can you imagine the way this guy asks—pleads —begs—cries—aches—moans—for a cup of coffee in the morning? Just try to picture him asking for a second mortgage.")

Not a pretty sight.

Among musicians, Real Men don't sample.

Real Men aren't into glam-rock. (And if you have to ask, don't worry: You're already a Real Man. These are the musicians who love fishnets, bare midriffs, teased hair, spiked heels, nail polish, and purple eyeliner—on themselves. The more appropriate terminology is "mousse rock.")

But on the other hand, Real Men do enjoy heavy metal. ("Real Men appreciate anything that can drown out a 747 at full power," said Flex. "But I keep waiting for a band to be named either Republican Guard, or Severe Tire Damage. I've even got the album names for Severe Tire Damage. First album: *Stop*. Second album: *Don't Back Up*. If that doesn't sound like something that ships double platinum, nothing does.")

And of course, Real Men will listen to anything by anybody named Keith Sweat.

So what's Flex Crush's favorite music?

"Country," he said. "Garth Brooks. Hank Williams. Randy Travis, Dwight Yoakam, Clint Black, Patsy Cline."

As Flex said this, the lights dimmed in the restaurant. A couple 'a the boys began to do a two-step in the corner. Fistfights broke out in the parking lot. Jealousy, lost love, and a longing for a simpler time hung in the air . . .

And Tiffany, poor child, wiped a single tear from her eye, and coulda sworn that four of the strangers at the counter were 1) her long-lost father, 2) her long-lost husband, 3) her long-lost momma, and 4) a fast-talkin' record producer from Nashville who was gonna promise to make her famous, and then break her little ole heart.

Out of nowhere, the Oak Ridge Boys and Alabama appeared, and began to hum.

Willie strummed on his only guitar the IRS hadn't hocked.

A lonesome train whistle blew in the distance; a thousand pickups turned off the road, headed down that dirt highway of hope.

We were all wearin' cowboy hats.

(I was also certain there was a dog howling somewhere in the restaurant, but I couldn't confirm it.)

"But Flex," I said, my accent suddenly heading 450 miles south, "why country?"

Flex took one last drag from his cigarette, and slipped another dollar in the CD-video jukebox.

"Because," he said. "Because only in country music could there be one song—and one song title—that explains the entire relationship between men and women—and exactly how men have felt about women —since the beginning of time."

"What's that?" I asked.

Flex smiled sadly.

"How Can I Miss You, When You Won't Go Away?"

"Remember bimbos?"

15
How to Create Your Own Real Man Movie

Y ou say it's another Friday night and there's not a single decent film to see?

You look in the paper, and the only thing playing at the local multiplex is *Steel Magnolias*?

On all twenty-six screens?

No Arnold, no Jean-Claude Van Damme, not a *single piece of footage* where a police car flies through a plate-glass window and flips over, crashing on its roof?

And the video store is out of everything except for an Angela Lansbury exercise tape and *City Slickers*?

("Hey! It's not that Real Men don't like Billy Crystal," Flex interrupted. "But there ought to be a limit to the number of epiphanies any one human being is allowed to have in one movie." Flex paused thoughtfully, and added: "Aside from that, there was only one thing wrong with *City Slickers*: Billy Crystal lived. Jack Palance died.")

Either way, put away that paper bag—there's no reason to hyperventilate, or hold up a 7-Eleven for cheap thrills. Because with Buddy-O-Matic, you can create Real Men movies right in the privacy of your own home. Yes, Real Men movies, with Real Men stars, just like in *Lethal Weapon, The Last Boy Scout, 48 HRS., White Nights, Running Scared, The Hard Way, Stakeout, Shakedown, Shoot to Kill, Off Limits, Thelma and Louise,* and any other film where it's Two Guys Against the System. And the best part is you can create 'em *whenever you want*—with all the gunplay, gratuitous nudity, and flying glass that Real Men demand in their cinematic *oeuvre.*

Just work your way through the fully annotated multiple-choice Buddy-O-Matic process, and like the best Real Men in the movies, you can't miss.

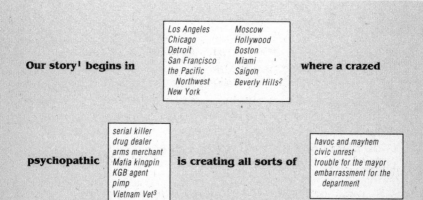

Our story[1] begins in

Los Angeles Moscow
Chicago Hollywood
Detroit Boston
San Francisco Miami
the Pacific Saigon
Northwest Beverly Hills[2]
New York

where a crazed

psychopathic

serial killer
drug dealer
arms merchant
Mafia kingpin
KGB agent
pimp
Vietnam Vet[3]

is creating all sorts of

havoc and mayhem
civic unrest
trouble for the mayor
embarrassment for the
department

1. The origins of the modern-day buddy movie (also known as the postheroic drama) are generally attributed to the 1969 film *Butch Cassidy and the Sundance Kid* (written by William Goldman), although the archetype had previously been employed by such premodernist comedy teams as Laurel and Hardy, and Abbott and Costello, along with the latter-day neo-expressionists Martin and Lewis. While scholars of the genre have failed to reach a consensus concerning the first appearance of the form, most agree the seminal influences include Shakespeare's *The Two Gentlemen of Verona,* the mythical Romulus and Remus, the biblical Cain and Abel, and, of course, the postwar Japanese-American classic *King Kong vs. Godzilla.*

2. If you're working on a budget (and who isn't these days?) Toronto is always available as the perfect stand-in/double for any of these cities. Just don't look too closely—especially if the action supposedly takes place in Saigon or Miami. Even then, chances are nobody will notice.

3. These are the all-purpose industrial-strength menaces; however if you feel "KGB agent" is archaic, feel free to substitute "power-crazed Japanese industrialist." Similarly, "Vietnam vet" can be modernized to "Desert Storm friendly-fire victim." And with the heightened awareness of black stereotypes, "pimp" may be changed to "investment banker." Of course, if you're truly determined not to offend *anyone,* there's only one safe choice: white upper-middle-class CEO. Use it, and no one will complain.

by murdering

> young nurses
> young models
> young hookers[4]

in a particularly

> lurid
> vicious
> sadistic
> bloody
> titillating[5]

style, and

for no apparent reason.[6] Next, we meet

Richard Dreyfuss	Mel Gibson
Billy Crystal	Jim Belushi
Michael Keaton	Tom Berenger
Michael J. Fox	Nick Nolte
Mikhail Baryshnikov	One of the Quaids[7]

who is a(n)

> down-and-out
> by-the-book
> soon-to-be-married
> wizened, seen-it-all
> alcoholic
> wrapped-too-tight

> sargeant
> detective
> MP
> FBI agent
> CIA operative
> ex–football star
> ballet dancer

who has just

> broken up with his girlfriend
> woken up with a hangover
> screwed up with the commissioner
> seen his partner get killed
> been dumped by his wife

in the

> sloppy bachelor's apartment
> middle-class two-family house
> slick high-tech loft[8]

he shares

---

4. Derived from the Roger Corman/American International Pictures school of film, beginning with *The Wild Angels* (1966), and later adapted to most Brian DePalma and *Nightmare on Elm Street* films. The important thing to remember here is that there seems to be a direct correlation between the amount of cleavage/danger shown on the poster, and the eventual box-office grosses. In other words, Real Men will risk anything—including political correctness and cash—for a scantily clad babe in dire straits.

5. True, these may seem like subtle differences, but for the true buddy film cineaste, the distinctions can mean all the differences between, say, *48 HRS.* and *Another 48 HRS.*

6. At this point in the story, it's essential that the reason for the killings remain unclear. The killer's motivation (known as the "big secret" or "final plot twist") is always revealed in the last ten minutes of the movie—except in the case of James Bond–derived films, where the "missing American atomic bomb" is always established up front.

7. Yes, all these guys have appeared in buddy films—and space prohibits listing, among others, Treat Williams, Clint Eastwood, Willem Dafoe, Judge Reinhold, and Dan Aykroyd. But if *none* of these choices make you happy, try Wesley Snipes or Woody Harrelson from the *White Men Can't Jump* urban basketball/gunslinger variation on the theme.

8. The "slick high-tech loft" only works in New York City, and even then, only in the set designer's dreams.

9. Known as the "Harvey trait" (after the 1950 James Stewart film *Harvey*), this is considered by screenwriters to be a fast and relatively easy way of giving sympathetic and endearing qualities to an otherwise cardboard character.

10. Again, any of these venues is acceptable; but if the film is set in Chicago, at least one scene must be set in the twin-towered circular multistoried indoor parking lot at the corner of State Street and the Chicago River. Additionally, a car must plunge from the sixth story of the aforesaid parking lot into the aforementioned river.

11. The phrases "Ex-Navy SEAL" or "former top gun pilot" may also be substituted at will. And for the European flavor, consider "cashiered MI-5 operative."

12. See note 5, but change *Another 48 HRS* to *Ishtar*.

13. Other choices include Sean Connery (*The Presidio*), Arnold (*Red Heat*), Burt Reynolds (*City Heat*), Shelley Long (*Outrageous Fortune*), and John Hurt (*Partners*). And if you're still not happy with any of these choices, consider substituting a dog for one of the partners, as in *K-9*, or *Turner and Hootch*.

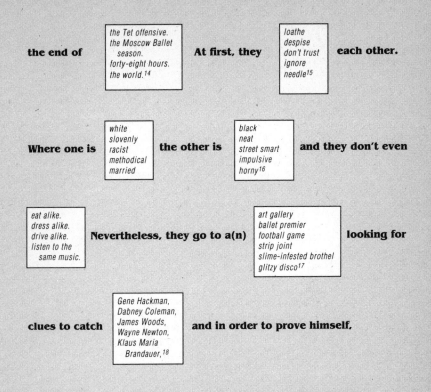

the end of

the Tet offensive.
the Moscow Ballet
  season.
forty-eight hours.
the world.[14]

At first, they

loathe
despise
don't trust
ignore
needle[15]

each other.

Where one is

white
slovenly
racist
methodical
married

the other is

black
neat
street smart
impulsive
horny[16]

and they don't even

eat alike.
dress alike.
drive alike.
listen to the
  same music.

Nevertheless, they go to a(n)

art gallery
ballet premier
football game
strip joint
slime-infested brothel
glitzy disco[17]

looking for

clues to catch

Gene Hackman,
Dabney Coleman,
James Woods,
Wayne Newton,
Klaus Maria
  Brandauer,[18]

and in order to prove himself,

14. This is known as the "ticking clock": a device that adds a sense of urgency, and means—essentially—that the movie has to be over by the end of the movie. Addtitional note: "The End of The World" is known as the "007 Gambit" and is only used in James Bond–derived films, and requires the establishment of the "missing thermonuclear device" just after the unprecedented-wave-of-gratuitous-violence sequence that precedes the opening credits.

15. See note 5, but change *Another 48 HRS.* to *Rain Man.*

16. Although listed here as single attributes for reasons of clarity, any combination or mixed usage is acceptable, per the Hope/Crosby rule of mutual antagonism, first cited in the "Road to . . ." series (1940), enlarged upon in *Stalag 17* (1953), and perfected in Neil Simon's *The Odd Couple* (1968). However, in the event a "multiple buddy" format is utilized (known as the "Dirty Dozen Formulation" or the "*Platoon* Template," each individual character must be given a single, easily recognized quirk/stereotype that will put him in constant conflict with the other members of his "buddy universe."

17. Don't discard "glitzy disco" out of hand: It's an excellent excuse to inject music from the forthcoming smash hit soundtrack album.

18. Although James Woods (and Willem Dafoe) have enjoyed co-hero status, both have also worked the other side of the buddy street. When in doubt, either makes a perfect crazed psychopath Vietnam vet/sullen-homicidal-maniac with a grudge, nothing-left-to-lose, no regrets, next time it's the chair/all-purpose, incorrigible, hard-case villain.

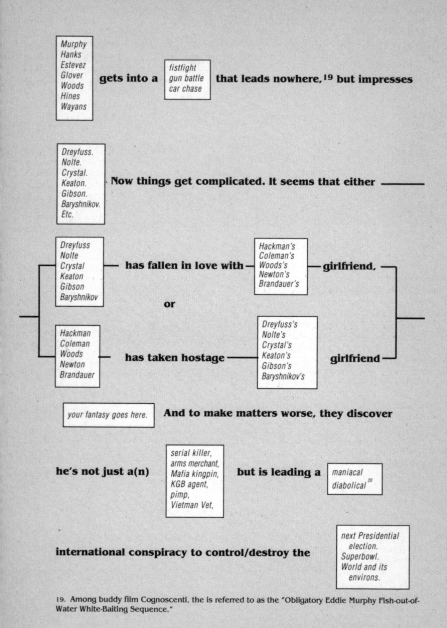

Murphy / Hanks / Estevez / Glover / Woods / Hines / Wayans **gets into a** fistfight / gun battle / car chase **that leads nowhere,[19] but impresses**

Dreyfuss. / Nolte. / Crystal. / Keaton. / Gibson. / Baryshnikov. / Etc. **Now things get complicated. It seems that either** ———

Dreyfuss / Nolte / Crystal / Keaton / Gibson / Baryshnikov **has fallen in love with** Hackman's / Coleman's / Woods's / Newton's / Brandauer's **girlfriend,**

or

Hackman / Coleman / Woods / Newton / Brandauer **has taken hostage** Dreyfuss's / Nolte's / Crystal's / Keaton's / Gibson's / Baryshnikov's **girlfriend**

your fantasy goes here. **And to make matters worse, they discover**

he's not just a(n) serial killer, / arms merchant, / Mafia kingpin, / KGB agent, / pimp, / Vietman Vet, **but is leading a** maniacal / diabolical[20]

international conspiracy to control/destroy the next Presidential election. / Superbowl. / World and its environs.

19. Among buddy film Cognoscenti, the is referred to as the "Obligatory Eddie Murphy Fish-out-of-Water White-Baiting Sequence."

20. A small semantic insight: Before Watergate, all grand schemes were called "diabolical"; after Nixon's resignation in 1974, they all became "maniacal." If you're creating a period piece buddy movie, it's attention to the details that counts.

Now, the heat is on. there's no way out. they're running scared.[21] **After another** car chase gun battle sex scene **with much** destruction of city property automatic weapons fire high-speed swerving and sheet metal carnage **either** Nolte saves Murphy. **or** Glover saves Gibson.[22] **At last, they realize how much they** like need respect **each other. And with** time running out, the bomb about to explode, the ballet curtain about to go up, **they use a combination of** street smarts and police know-how **or** police know-how and street smarts[23] **to appropriate a** cement truck Greyhound bus Ferrari[24] **and engage in another** gun battle car chase sex scene **through** the Chicago subway system, the Kremlin, a Chinese New Year parade, the Miami intercoastal waterway, the atrium of a Hyatt Hotel, Mardi Gras,[25] **where they kill** Gene Hackman, Dabney Coleman, James Woods, Wayne Newton, Klaus Maria Brandauer, **save** your fantasy goes here, **and make Lou Gossett very happy, but not before the last scene, where** Richard Dreyfuss / Billy Crystal / Michael Keaton / Michael J. Fox / Mikhail Baryshnikov / Mel Gibson / Jim Belushi / Tom Berenger / Nick Nolte / One of the Quaids **turns to**

---

21. It's always nice to work in the title at some point in the film. (Also, see note 17, and get Phil Collins on the phone.)

22. Actually, it doesn't matter who saves who, so long as some kind of ritualistic death-cheating scene takes place to formalize the all-important "buddy" process. The Rosetta stone of all these scenes is the Butch Cassidy cliff-jumping sequence.

23. If you're thinking about Europe, use "American can-do" and "British savoir faire."

24. This is known as the Rule of Incongruous Transportation. Any vehicle will do, as long as it's completely anomalous. In *Beverly Hills Cop II* it's a cement truck on Santa Monica Boulevard; in *Running Scared*, a car on the Chicago subway tracks. The only exception to this rule takes place in New York City, where nothing seems incongruous.

25. It actually doesn't matter what, or where, so long as it's bigger, longer, louder, and deadlier than the previous gun battle/car chase.

Eddie Murphy
Tom Hanks
Emilio Estevez
Danny Glover
James Woods
Gregory Hines
Damon Wayans[26]

and scowls,

"Later."
"See ya."
"Trust me."
"Can I have my
   lighter back?"[27]

before driving off into

Los Angeles.	Moscow.
Chicago.	Hollywood.
Detroit.	Boston.
San Francisco.	Miami.
the Pacific Northwest.	Saigon.
New York.	Beverly Hills.[28]

26. Even though we're at the end of the story, you needn't feel limited to these choices the next time you play. Be goofy. How about . . . Telly Savalas and Garrison Keillor? Call it "Telly & Gar." Telly: "Who loves you, baby?" Gar: "Well . . . Ummm . . . Gee. I'd have to think about that."

27. The operative word here is *cool*. No matter what our heroes say, it must be totally unemotional, and manly. If all else fails, they can punch each other. (For the perfect realization of this scenario, see *Rocky II*, wherein Rocky Balboa climbs back into the ring with Apollo Creed for a poignant, friendly, man-to-man sparring contest.)

28. While buddy movie traditionalists prefer "the sunset," those seeking a more contemporary feeling would do well to use the ending currently favored by Hollywood, known, of course, as "the sequel."

16

The Real Man's Unified Theory of the Cosmos

For eons, men have looked to the skies for answers.

How did it start?

How did we get here?

Why are we stuck in this traffic jam when there's no visible reason for it?

Quarks, black holes, supernovas, strings, the weak force—we search the heavens for understanding.

Quantum mechanics, the space-time continuum, the big bang theory, the uncertainty principle, the no-hair theorem, the thermodynamic arrow of time—we try to resolve our place in the universe.

Einstein, Newton, Darwin, Bohr, Hawking, Feynman, Rubbia, van der Meer, Kirk—the greatest minds of their times have peered into the chaos, looking for order.

Yet Real Men have always known the answer.

For in their heart of hearts, they've always perceived there's one guiding principle that governs everything, from the galaxies, to the planets, to the fate of John Sununu, and Drexel Burnham going bankrupt.

"What goes around, comes around."

17
The Real Man's Guide to Safe Sex

1. Wear a condom.
2. Marry young.
3. Marry rich.

18
Real Women

- Real women are not congenitally late.
- A Real Woman will initiate things in the bedroom at least 50 percent of the time.
- Real Women don't secretly record your phone calls.
- And then sell them to the *Star*.
- And then take cash to talk about it on "A Current Affair."
- But on the other hand, a Real Woman would have booted Gary Hart's ass out of the house, pronto.
- Real Women are smart enough to make friends with your family and friends—if only out of self-protection. (She knows these are the first people you'll turn to for advice in the event of a major fight, and she wants them on her side.)
- Real Women will go to your insanely boring six-hour business dinners—*and* charm the tie/pearls off your boss—but only if you're willing to do the same at her insanely boring six-hour business dinners.
- Real Women are still pissed off that the business accolades "tough, performance-oriented, and no-nonsense" translate to "bitch" when applied to a female.

"Your primal mother is talking to you!"

- A Real Woman would laugh absurdly at the idea of "needing to get in touch with her femininity."
- And as we all know, in their previous lives, all Real Women were once Real Men.

"... and finally may I say to my colleagues on
the board—in the words of Johnny Paycheck—
'Take this job and shove it.'"

19
Real Man Quiz #4 The Final Exam: Compare and Contrast

Close your eyes for a moment.

Picture a glorious ten-point day in Santa Monica, California. The Pacific glitters in the distance; the sky is an endless panorama of cockpit blue.

As you turn around, you spot a guy on the street. He's about thirty. Balding. What's left of his hair is pulled back in a ponytail. He's wearing a twelve-hundred-dollar Armani suit, a T-shirt, and sunglasses. He's on rollerblades. There's a cellular telephone glued to his left ear, over which he's trying to negotiate the cable TV movie rights to an amateur video-tape of sixty-three cops beating up on a presidential candidate for jaywalking on a street in downtown L.A. while he was having sex with his mistress.

And if the deal doesn't go through, the guy's thinking about suing the city for "stress-related" injuries incurred by watching the tape.

This is not a Real Man.

Now wipe that picture out of your mind.

Think about snow. Seven feet of snow. Seven feet of oppressive, heavy, wet, gray snow, under an oppressive, heavy, murder/suicide gray sky. In February. At the airport in Bismarck, North Dakota, where the wind-chill factor is $-130°$, and the video screens say that all departures have been temporarily delayed. Until June.

How do you spot the Real Man?

Look over at the phone carousel.

He—or she—is the one in the rumpled overcoat, with the wet shoes, the bulging briefcase, and the battered carry-on hanging bag, trying to make the only connection that really matters:

The next flight home.

20

Flex Crush, and the Short Good-bye

*D*awn was breaking over the Vince Lombardi Rest Area on the Jersey Turnpike.

The sky had turned a hellish-purple gray; the thunder of the big rigs—the eighteen-wheelers, the semis, the triple-tandem tractors—reverberated through the parking lot.

For better or for worse, it was, as Ronald Reagan once said, morning in America.

Flex had paid the check, and we were now all standing on the asphalt beside his truck: Tiffany, the Oak Ridge Boys, the two goons who buried Hoffa, and half a dozen guys getting an early jump on the 1996 Democratic presidential campaign, all of whom wanted Flex's endorsement.

Flex ignored the candidates.

"This whole men's movement is just so much non-sense," he said at last. "There is no such thing as the 'new man.'

"For the best of us, it's just the same old man adapting, changing, putting one foot in front of the other, trying to find his way."

Flex smiled, and much to my surprise, quoted

something he remembered reading in high school by John Donne.

"Hey," he said with a shrug. "We work in the dark. We do what we can."

Flex kissed Tiffany on the cheek, checked the zipper on his Levis, yanked the lawyer out from under the front wheels, and pulled himself up into the cab of the Peterbilt.

I considered saying something about the night's events, but in true Real Man style, decided against it.

We both understood.

"Just remember one thing," Flex said, pulling the door shut behind him.

"Bonding is like the romance in an Arnold Schwarzenegger movie.

"If it happens along the way, fine.

"But it ain't the reason you go there."